A Bulletproof™

M000216870

The Bulletproof™
Firearms Business

The Legal Secrets
to Success Under Fire

BENNET K. LANGLOTZ

ANGELA V. LANGLOTZ

Arbogast Publishing, LLC

Copies of this book may be obtained for educational, business, or promotional uses. For more information, contact Special Market Sales, Arbogast Publishing, LLC, PO Box 759 Genoa, NV 89411

Copyright ©2008 Arbogast Property Management, LLC
All Rights Reserved

Published by Arbogast Publishing, LLC, PO Box 759 Genoa, NV 89411

Printed in the United States of America

Second Printing

ISBN 978-0-9815254-0-2

In Memory of John B. Williams, Jr.,
who invited us to our first SHOT Show, and whose early
encouragement helped us reach toward success.

TABLE OF CONTENTS

About the Authors

Bennet K. Langlotz is a Patent and Trademark Attorney specializing in the firearms industry. His writings on firearms and law have appeared in *Small Arms Review* magazine, *The Washington Post*, and *The Washington Times*. A Stanford University engineering graduate, he is an avid firearms enthusiast, and has 20 years of experience in the patent and trademark fields.

Ben's favorite guns include a 50BMG take-down target rifle that gets far too little use (and is the "wrong" brand—sorry Ronnie!) Ben's favorite gun he actually shoots on a regular basis is an integrally suppressed 22LR with a US Optics 1–4x scope. It leans against the wall next to his desk for purposes of protecting the bird feeder from marauding ground squirrels.

Ben is also the inventor of the patented "Trigger Tamer" drop-in part that reduces the Steyr AUG's heavy trigger pull by one-third.

He may be contacted at bennet@langlotz.com

Angela V. Langlotz is an Estate Planning and Asset Protection Attorney specializing in the firearms industry. Her writings have appeared in *The Tax Lawyer*, the scholarly publication of the American Bar Association Taxation Section. She teaches at estate planning and business law seminars for her fellow attorneys. Angela is admitted to practice law in Nevada, California, Wyoming, Washington, and Oregon. She has litigated at the appellate level as a legal activist on behalf of firearms rights.

When asked to list her favorite firearms, Angela says, "I'm kinda boring, I mostly like pistols." But in addition to her preferred compact stainless-steel carry gun (note that non-clients don't get a mention) she has a fondness for the curvaceous family AUG, and likes to consider it her own.

She may be contacted at angela@langlotz.com

Why We Wrote This Book

In a remarkable coincidence, on the same day I sat down to write these words, I got a profound reminder of just why we wrote this book.

I got a call from a recent client that makes some of the hottest, most drool-inducing military rifles around, the kind of fun guns that give Chuck Schumer and Hillary Clinton the night sweats.

They're a well-run company with talented personnel. You've probably seen their impressive SHOT Show booth in recent years. I filed a patent application for them last year, and I've been bugging them about trademarks ever since.

Today, the president of the company called, and I bugged him about trademarks again. He agreed it was time, so I did a little checking on his website to make a list of all the brands that needed protecting. Turns out, they hadn't even registered the company name that's stamped on every rifle they make! But that's not the worst of it.

I found about a dozen unprotected trademarks, including one for a new .30 caliber rifle I really want. I did a quick trademark search for that brand name and got bad news: A similar mark is already registered for similar goods. My client has been investing in someone else's brand!

Now, I've gotta break the bad news: He needs to scrap the brand name for the rifle everybody wants and start his marketing from scratch. I guess it could've been worse—at least he didn't find out about this in a lawsuit complaint.

But he could have avoided the disaster simply by sending me a quick email when he picked the new brand, *before* he started using it. I would have done a quick search, found the conflict, and advised him to pick another brand.

This kind of thing happens all the time, oftentimes to some excellent companies run by smart guys.

Update: weeks after this was written, I visited my client's booth at the SHOT Show, and learned that the president had been terminated by the new owner/investor. Draw your own conclusions.

Other companies end up tangled up in a trademark lawsuit, all because they failed to register their own trademarks.

Avoidable legal disaster happens on the patent side too.

Sometimes I'll be visiting a friendly booth at the SHOT Show, and learn from the boss that they've got a great invention they want to patent. Finally, a big one that justifies the investment in a patent.

Everything is great, until my questioning reveals that the invention's been on the market for more than a year, meaning that they permanently blew the chance to protect their valuable innovation.

They just gave away the crown jewels to their worst competition.

A needless lawsuit may be a temporary waste of money and time, but losing patent rights is forever.

My co-author and wife Angela has similar stories about smart firearms companies that leave themselves wide open to lawsuits by failing to protect their assets.

Like the dear friend and client whose company in our industry was sued. It turned out that he'd set up his company in a way that put all his own personal assets in jeopardy. He had no idea that a little planning and structuring could have kept not just his personal assets protected, but also his critical business assets.

It would've been possible for him to keep essential business assets like patents and trademarks away from the predatory trial lawyers. But by the time the lawsuit was filed, it was too late to protect anything.

If he'd set things up right in advance, the trial lawyers probably wouldn't even have bothered to sue.

That's why we wrote this book. We want to prevent any more needless legal disasters like these, especially for clients we respect so much for their contribution to an industry that's so important to our liberty.

We want our readers to know what is *possible* to achieve with smart Bulletproof legal strategies.

The billionaires know what's possible, but few smart business owners or their general lawyers are aware of the powerful legal tools that exist to secure and protect their assets.

The key is a little education that tells you what it's possible to achieve, and how simple it is to do it. You can easily implement procedures for ensuring your business grows securely against all the risks that too many firearms businesses ignore.

The first section of this book is about Trademarks and will help you protect your brands and stay out of trademark lawsuits.

The second section is about Patents, to help you protect your innovations. Even if you think you're not high-tech, you'll be surprised what's patentable.

The third section is about Business Structuring and Asset Protection. If you learn how to build asset value in the first two sections, you'll learn how to *keep* it in the third section.

We sincerely hope that reading this book puts you on a path to greater prosperity and security, beyond what you imagined was possible.

Ben and Angela Langlotz
January 2008

Section I:
TRADEMARKS

Chapter 1

The Three Things I Wish Every Business Owner Knew About Trademarks

1. SEARCH FIRST.

It's suicidal (and all too common) to start using new brands without *first* doing a trademark search.

2. REGISTER YOUR TRADEMARKS.

Registering your trademarks increases asset value and helps you avoid ruinous lawsuits.

3. USE YOUR TRADEMARKS CAREFULLY.

Using your trademarks the wrong way can undermine your rights. It's easy to get it right, but you're probably getting it dangerously wrong until you learn the rules.

Chapter 2

They Failed to Search,
They Lost the Company

The Trademark Search
That Could Have Saved a Fortune

In the middle of last year, I got a call from a client who owns a successful small company in the firearms industry. They'd been distributing their game scent attractant regionally for a couple of years.

They'd started to hit it big, with major contracts from big hunting retailers like Cabela's. They ramped up production and were "printing money," with a warehouse full of product that would easily sell and make the owners a continuing fortune.

Then, they got an angry letter from lawyers of a big company, telling them that their game scent trademark infringes their ammunition trademark. Because the marks are similar and the goods are related (sold through similar channels to a similar market), my new client got bad news: Stop using the trademark, chuck all the inventory, and then hope you still don't get sued for past damages.

I managed to negotiate an agreement with the big trademark owner that kept my client alive: My client could sell out his existing labeled inventory over the next 6 months, put up disclaimers on the website, notify his customers about the issue (embarrassing) and sign an agreement never to come near the big company's trademark again.

So my client didn't quite go bankrupt. But they were then faced with starting a new brand from scratch, regaining the reputation and recognition for a good product, and overcoming the inevitable confusion among consumers who faced the new product with a different brand name.

Failure to search for trademark conflicts before adopting a trademark meant bare survival, not earned success.

The first and foremost rule of trademarks is:

> # NEVER USE A TRADEMARK WITHOUT SEARCHING IT FIRST.

Here's an even bigger trademark disaster:

The 60-Second Trademark Search That Could Have Prevented Bankruptcy

Another client of mine was a small video production company, about to launch a big new educational DVD set under a new brand name. They'd proudly secured a great domain name, created an impressive website, were implementing a solid marketing strategy, and had a warehouse of quality inventory ready to ship.

They came to me to register their brand name to protect against infringers (smart move, but bad timing). About 60 seconds later, after punching some tiny buttons on my Blackberry, I told them the bad news: The brand name they had picked infringed someone else's trademark.

Their jaws dropped as I explained that they couldn't even legally use their own Internet domain name.

They couldn't use the packaging for the product.

They couldn't use the preprinted DVDs.

The content of the DVDs kept referring to a brand name that wasn't theirs to use. That meant scrapping the inventory, rerecording the entire production, and starting from scratch.

All this sent their business into the bankruptcy dumpster, along with their entire inventory, simply because they didn't get trademark advice when they really needed it.

They failed to search a trademark before starting to use it.

The Good News:
Trademark Searching is Fast And Affordable

Trademark law may be a narrow specialty, but a trademark search is a quick and easy matter.

Just email your attorney with a short list of proposed brands, and the types of products they'll be used on. In a few days, maybe hours, you'll get a reply telling you which brands are clear to proceed.

All that for hundreds of dollars, not thousands.

Can you imagine any smart business owner knowing this, and NOT having new brands searched for trademark clearance?

Later in this section, we'll cover searching in greater detail. But all you really need to know is that it's business insanity not to search each and every one of your new brands before you start using them.

Chapter 3

Tales of Disaster:
Failure to Register Trademarks

Squeezed Out by the Big Guys Over an Unregistered Trademark

A client of mine was operating on a shoestring at the early stages. He wasn't stupid, so he had me search any new brands before he started using them.

He'd also heard that you can still have "common law" unregistered trademark rights even without paying a penny to register the trademarks.

Unfortunately, those unregistered trademarks may be "free," but they aren't cheap.

My client was growing, and doing well, but with a low profile. He'd done business in a few states, and was getting ready to expand nationwide.

Unfortunately, a big, respectable company picked a similar trademark for similar goods, and did a thorough trademark search to make sure *they* didn't find themselves on the wrong end of a trademark lawsuit.

But the big company's trademark search didn't find my client's trademark. It wasn't in the federal search database to find, because my client had never applied to register it. So the big guys innocently adopted their new brand, and invested in it nationwide.

Bad news for my "shoestring" client. Because even though he used the mark first, his rights are limited only to the areas where he actually used the trademark. The big guys earned rights to the entire rest of the nation, either by using it nationwide, or more likely, simply by filing an application to register the mark.

So my client can't expand his business beyond a couple of states, unless he picks a new brand. Of course, he can keep the big guys out of his small territory, and maybe they'll buy out his rights. Or maybe the big guys will just bluster in to my client's territory, knowing that the little guy couldn't possibly fund a trademark lawsuit.

All of this could probably have been avoided if my client had applied to register his trademark as early as possible. Filing to register a trademark secures instant nationwide rights, even if the nationwide expansion takes a long time, even decades.

If my shoestring client had been in the registration database, the big guys would have found him. They would have been steered off, and been smart enough simply to pick another brand. But once the big guys had invested so much in advertising their trademark, they were much more likely to fight for it.

If you can steer them out of your territory before they stumble in, you can avoid the conflict in the first place.

Filing to register a trademark is a little like fencing in your ranch with barbed wire. Not only does it help secure your property (cattle, trademarks) but it provides the added benefits of helping to keep accidental trespassers (infringers) off your turf.

Embroiled in Litigation Because They Failed to Register a Trademark

A winning legal position can be a losing business position.

Another client of mine failed to register an important trademark, but at least they used it nationwide in online sales, so they had rights throughout the nation. Problem solved, right? No need to worry about losing out to a fast-expanding competitor, because he had nationwide rights?

No, having unregistered trademark rights doesn't mean you're safe.

Just like the first example, another big company unknowingly picked a conflicting trademark. The big company invested in their trademark and was motivated to do what it took to be able to keep using it. With no easy way out, they were like a cornered rat. Willing to fight. Expensively.

Now, the big guys are supposed to lose here. That's what the law says. But in the real world of trademark litigation, there are always debatable points, and the big guys usually put up a tough, confident front.

Maybe they hope that my client can't afford litigation and will fold. Maybe they find that he's been sloppy about how he uses his trademark, and can challenge the trademark rights that way (see this book's critical chapter on trademark usage to avoid important pitfalls).

In this case, the big guys found one of dozens of other legal challenges that my client left open by not getting basic legal advice early on, and registering the trademark as they should have. The challenges may be weak, but the big guys could afford endless litigation to grind down my client, even if the issues have little or no merit.

So, do you think my shoestring client who couldn't afford to invest a few thousand dollars registering trademarks could afford *hundreds of thousands* in trademark litigation legal fees?

No, they had to roll over. And it's worse to roll over knowing that you were in the right.

All this trouble would've been avoided if my client had simply registered their trademark, so it would have appeared in the searchable database for the other guy to avoid.

So, do you think that my client registers its important brands now?

A Trademark Registration That Could Have Saved a Fortune in Litigation Costs

Another client owned an unregistered trademark, and when an infringer came around, my client decided he'd had enough and sued to enforce his trademark rights.

Unfortunately, my client found out that his lawsuit bills were much more than expected (I don't litigate, but I helped him find a good firm). The other side contested whether the trademark really was eligible for trademark protection for a host of reasons.

There were days of depositions and trial on issues that would have been resolved in advance by a trademark examiner granting a registration.

Judges may think they're geniuses, but they don't think of themselves as trademark experts, and when they see that an unbiased trademark examiner with extensive training and experience has ruled that your trademark meets all legal standards, then they tend to dismiss the infringer's arguments to the contrary. Luckily, none of those extraneous issues went against my client.

So, my client "won" the lawsuit (didn't collect a penny) and his legal bills were in the six figure range, maybe double what they would have been. And he spent added months losing sleep and being distracted from the primary focus of running his business to generate a profit.

If my client had registered the brand, the other guys probably would never have stepped into the conflict, and there would have been no lawsuit.

And if that infringer was one of those irresponsible businesses that doesn't even search trademarks? A registration would not have prevented litigation. But it would have made the litigation quicker, more affordable, and more winnable.

Registering your trademarks makes suing for infringement easier and cheaper, and leaves fewer arguments for the infringer to attack your rights.

Registered Trademarks Strengthen Your Negotiation Position in a Conflict

Another client had an unregistered trademark they used nationwide. An infringer had adopted the same mark for similar goods, because my client's trademark didn't show up in the Patent and Trademark Office database.

Then, we faced a serious negotiation to try to resolve the conflict without expensive litigation.

In any negotiation, each side tries to estimate the probability and pain of each possible outcome if the case went to court.

Because my client's trademark was unregistered, the other lawyer kept hitting us with all kinds of real and imagined arguments of why we had no trademark rights and would lose at trial.

Most of those arguments would have been irrelevant if we were talking about a registered trademark, because the trademark examiner that granted the registration would've already resolved the issues in our favor.

The infringer knew that it would be much tougher for my client to win a lawsuit on his unregistered mark. This made the infringer a little cockier and he drove a more stubborn bargain to settle the issue. The infringer knew that the lawsuit would be more expensive and riskier for my client.

In the end, the infringer of the unregistered trademark offered to pay a small royalty to continue his use of the mark, but the royalty was well below what it would have been if my client had registered the mark. It really didn't adequately compensate my client for the effect of having another trademark user out there competing with him.

The investment in registering the trademark would have been minuscule compared to the financial benefits of a stronger negotiating position.

Good news: It's Never Too Late to Register Your Trademarks

Ideally, you register your trademarks before you start using them (more on that strategy later). But even if you have a pile of unregistered trademarks, it's never too late to get your ducks in a row.

If you've been lucky enough to avoid trademark conflicts over your unregistered marks, you can still gain all the lawsuit-avoiding benefits of registration at any time. The sooner the better.

It's kind of like health insurance. If someone went uninsured for years, but stayed healthy, it still makes sense for them to protect themselves starting now.

Fortunately, trademark registrations aren't terribly expensive. And once you have a trademark attorney on your team, a new registration takes little more effort than a quick email.

Later in this section, we'll cover all the details of the registration process.

Chapter 4

To Register or Not to Register?

Unregistered Trademarks—"Free" but not Cheap

"Common law" trademarks are trademarks that aren't registered with the Patent and Trademark Office. They give minimal legal rights just by using them, but don't give the many benefits of registration.

The big problem is that a common law mark can't be found in the Patent and Trademark Office (PTO) database.

Another problem with an unregistered trademark is that it gives only localized rights where the mark was actually used or where sales occurred. That gives competitors a chance to gain rights where the mark hasn't yet been used. Which can keep you from expanding your business into other territories.

And an unregistered trademark hasn't received a stamp of approval from a trademark examiner. The examiner is an attorney who grants a registration only when, in his unbiased opinion, all legal tests have been met. Judges respect this. Therefore, unregistered trademarks have less credibility in legal conflicts, making negotiation and litigation uphill battles.

Chapter 5

The Powerful Advantages of Federal Registration

It bears repeating. It's one of the most important messages of this book. There are profound advantages to registering your trademarks. I've never met someone who regretted getting a trademark registration.

Registration Advantage #1:
Nationwide Trademark Rights—Instantly

An application for federal trademark registration secures nationwide rights, instantly.

The moment the application is filed, you've tied up rights nationwide, even if it takes a year or more for your registration to be granted.

That means *even if you haven't yet used your trademark,* or only in a limited area, simply filing an application for registration secures the whole nation.

That prevents other competitors from cropping up in places you don't know about and using your mark before you've actually had the chance to expand into those areas.

Registration Advantage #2:
A Registration Steers Competitors Away From Your Trademark Rights, Preventing Lawsuits

Filing to register your trademark helps competitors avoid adopting conflicting marks. I believe that this is one of the most important advantages of registration.

Normally, we don't like helping our competitors, but in this instance, it helps us even more than it helps them. We don't want our competitors getting themselves backed into a corner with a conflicting trademark that leads to litigation.

When you apply for a mark, your application is entered into the searchable database. That occurs immediately, even before it's registered, making it very easy for a competitor to search to find the mark that you're using or planning to use.

When you've applied for registration, competitors have a chance to evaluate your rights, and apply the same kind of conservative conflict-avoidance principles that we would use when deciding whether a new trademark was safe to adopt. This helps them to avoid adopting a mark similar to yours and keeps both sides from getting embroiled in a trademark lawsuit.

If you have a common-law mark that you didn't apply to register, then even when a competitor does his best to search for a conflicting mark, they won't find it (remember, your common law mark isn't in the database). Finding no conflicts, they adopt what they think is a perfectly good, safe mark.

You'll learn about their conflicting mark only later, after they've invested in the mark. They're entrenched, and now they have something worth fighting for. They may have invested millions promoting the mark. Now they're much more likely to be willing to litigate, even if it's a borderline case, because they can't afford to just let the mark go.

So now you're forced either to let them have the trademark, even though they don't have the legal right to it, or to pay big bucks to go through the litigation.

Believe me, you don't want to be here. Thankfully, a registration helps keep you out of this kind of conflict.

Registration Advantage #3:
Getting Your Trademark Into the Database Makes
Trademark Examiners Your Watchdogs

Getting into the database doesn't just help your competitors avoid stepping on your rights, it also helps keep trademark examiners from granting conflicting registrations to your competitors.

You don't want a competitor to get a registration for a mark that's similar to yours. That's because a registration gives them certain legal presumptions that strengthen their position.

Here's what you do want to happen: You want a trademark examiner to find your registered (or applied for) trademark in the database, and to use that against the application of a competitor to hold them at bay.

Basically, you want to put that trademark examiner to work for you, using your registered mark as ammunition against all those who would come up against you with similar marks.

That doesn't cost you anything extra once you're in the database. And your application gets you into the database instantly and permanently.

The sooner the better.

Registration Advantage #4:
The Power of a Registration Strengthens Your Legal Position

Another advantage of registration is that a more credible legal threat helps to resolve conflicts more quickly.

You're carrying a "bigger stick."

Let's say that someone turns out to be infringing my client's trademark. I write the infringer a letter accusing them of infringement and demanding they cease using the mark. I do this whether or not my client's mark is registered.

But my threat is not going to be taken as seriously with an unregistered trademark.

If we ever did have to litigate an unregistered trademark, we'd have a whole bunch more hurdles to prove in court. Imagine the cost to add extra court days and extra depositions.

Having a registration streamlines litigation, so there's less for you to prove at trial. It saves you money.

A registration is also more likely to win the lawsuit, because there are fewer issues on which a judge can rule against you.

Registration of your mark means that someone's going to take my cease-and-desist letter more seriously. They'll know they're up against a tougher case. They have a greater risk of losing any litigation, so they're going to be much more agreeable to a negotiation than they would be if you only had an unregistered trademark.

A registered trademark has been examined by an unbiased, specialized trademark lawyer who has concluded that your trademark meets all the legal tests. If you don't have a registered trademark when you go to court, you're going to have to convince the judge that your trademark is legitimate—and believe me, your litigation opponents are going to try to convince the judge otherwise.

Costs and Risks of Registration

The cost to invest in trademark registrations is usually only a minor disadvantage of registering trademarks. Trademark registration is a fairly-low budget item compared to other legal services, but it isn't free.

Depending on whether you select a low-end internet source (who may or may not be a lawyer) or a top trademark attorney, you can budget roughly $500–2000 to get a trademark registered. Long term maintenance and renewal costs work out to less than $100 per year per registration. So, most businesses will weigh the importance of each brand they propose to register, and if protecting it justifies the modest investment, they'll register it.

There's another important and subtle disadvantage to trademark registration. It's not even a disadvantage of registration per se. It's a risk of filing for registration without having first searched for the trademark to make sure you don't infringe someone else's rights.

It comes up only once in a while, but it's something you need to know about. As much as trademark registration makes sense in just about every case, and for just about every business, this one disadvantage is one you need to take seriously. It's the "lightning rod" theory.

The most serious trademark owners (we discuss these "Police Dogs" in a later chapter) are continually monitoring the trademark database for new applications for similar marks that might conflict with their crown jewel trademarks. When a mark with certain terms comes up, they may have a program in place that flags it and starts the "cease-and-desist" process. However, those efforts don't usually search for unregistered trademarks, so they usually slip under the radar, at least for a time.

This is a particular concern when my client is already using the mark or plans to invest heavily in the mark, and it would be painful to discontinue using the mark. In these situations, we want to make sure to conduct a thorough search for conflicting marks, and analyze the potential conflicts conservatively. Because if the owner of a conflicting trademark turns out to be policing their trademark rights, your application could trigger them into legal action, which might never have happened if you had laid low.

Other than that one risk, which can be effectively minimized by the kind of search I routinely conduct as a prerequisite to filing a trademark application, the profound advantages of trademark registration remain.

Chapter 6

The Value of Trademarks

Imagine a world without trademarks. Suppose you put out a good product, but customers had no way of knowing who produced it? Even if they wanted to buy from you again, they couldn't be sure whether a product was one of your typical high-quality products or a competitor's junk. In that kind of world, all the quality businesses would be driven out by the junk-makers.

Trademarks are all about reputation. Even without using a brand name, "the guy who sells the good firewood parks his truck on that corner on Saturdays" serves as a way for consumers to identify the source of the goods. That firewood guy can charge a premium as his reputation grows.

But other guys may catch on and park there and try to sell to customers who think they're buying from the guy with the good firewood. So our quality seller does something more to identify himself. Maybe he's known as "the guy in the blue truck." Or is known by his name: "Fred." Better still, he puts up a sign: "Fred's Firewood."

Now, Fred gets the benefit of a trademark. But it took Fred years to catch on to this, so he probably lost a lot of business. He should have decided right at the start to create a brand and let that brand (trademark) become immediately associated with quality firewood. The value starts building, and even if Fred should become disabled in a few years, he could sell the business and the right to use that brand to someone else. Without a trademark, no one would buy his business because they could just sell firewood on their own without paying Fred a penny. What's to buy?

A trademark is like a bucket that stores all the value of your business reputation. That value can be built over time by delivering quality products or services and can be enhanced by investing in advertising and other marketing efforts.

Key Trademark Mistakes Businesses Make

Amazingly, some companies pour their massive marketing investment into a rusty, leaky bucket. They use trademarks that were never cleared with a simple search and eventually may have to be abandoned (wasting all that advertising investment).

Too many companies fail to register their important brands. Thus, they miss an opportunity to avoid lawsuits, to strengthen their rights, and to build their business value.

Others misuse their trademarks in a sloppy, dangerous way that can kill what would have been good trademark rights.

And these aren't just start-up businesses. They're serious, established companies that are respected in their industries. But they've typically neglected one of their most critical categories of business assets.

It's not because they can't afford the nominal costs. Imagine the short-sighted companies that don't even spend 1% of their ad budget on the legal services it takes to protect the brands they're promoting! They're like a rancher who risks losing his valuable herd because he didn't bother to buy a gate for the corral.

No, too many business owners and executives are simply unaware of how important trademark protection is. Others are vaguely aware, but don't know what to do about it right now, and they think they have better things to do than dig through the yellow pages looking for a trademark attorney.

And too many trademark attorneys neglect their own clients' real needs. They're busy with other things, and simply wait for the client to call with a request for a trademark search or registration, instead of taking an active strategic involvement to help the client build a trademark portfolio of significant enduring value.

If you want Bulletproof trademarks, you need that kind of Bulletproof service.

What Part of a $100,000,000 Business Price Tag Do You Think Trademarks Represented?

Let me tell you a real story from my own law practice. A firearms industry client of mine was acquired for over $100,000,000. It was a friendly, good-news buyout with a staggering price tag. Industry insiders can probably figure out who it was.

I certainly won't take credit for that price tag, but I have to believe that, like lots of others on their team, the things I had done for their trademark portfolio over the prior couple of years helped raise their business value at least a little bit. And a little bit of that hefty price tag is still a lot!

Here's how I helped my client realize their extraordinary business goals: Some years back, I met the key players of the company at their giant SHOT Show booth. Coming back to say hello a few years later, they told me they needed someone like me to handle their patent and trademark work. Their old patent and trademark attorney wasn't being an active part of their team, and they were growing so fast they needed some real help.

I analyzed their current brand portfolio, told them about the benefits of registering their important brands, and quietly proceeded to secure them an impressive trademark portfolio. I educated their key employees, and established systems that made it easy for them to ensure that nothing fell through the cracks.

But here's the important part: Instead of just waiting until they called me up with a new brand to protect, I added another strategy. Without being asked, I studied their catalog, and researched the trademark database, so I could give them some important advice.

I generated a list of their brands that they had neglected to protect with a federal registration, and asked them which ones they thought were worth investing in. Some weren't important or were likely to be discontinued. But others were critical brands that were sitting unprotected. We fixed that in short order, and the registered or pending trademark portfolio became several times larger than it had been when we started.

By giving my client Bulletproof trademark service, I helped them secure a portfolio of brands that made sure nothing fell through the cracks. That maximizes business asset value.

Chapter 7

Trademark Basics in Brief

This book is intended for a busy executive who's not looking to become a trademark expert. I assume the reader understands the fundamentals of what a trademark is. A later part of this section will provide much greater detail for those wanting to better understand the trademark process and the principles behind trademark law. That will answer the kinds of questions my clients often ask me as they go through the process.

Meanwhile, let me give you a bullet list of key trademark principles (and there will be exceptions to many of them):

- Trademarks are typically words ("Nike," "Jaguar") or images (the Chevrolet "bow-tie," the Apple "apple") that help identify the source or origin of goods or services.

- Trademark rights arise only from *using* a trademark. If you stop using a trademark, it dies. If you keep using it, it can live forever. For instance, Coca Cola never needs to worry about their trademark expiring. If you stop using it for more than a short time, then someone else can later start using the same trademark.

- Trademark rights are limited only to related goods and services (which explains the coexistence of United Airlines, United Van Lines, and United Furniture Rental). Normally, your trademark rights do not extend outside of your own industry category.

- Trademark Rights are geographically limited to the area where the mark is actually used. But registering a trademark can overcome this limitation.

- Owners of unregistered trademarks still have "common law" rights, but these are weaker than the rights of a registered trademark.

Congratulations! You just graduated from the "CliffsNotes" (yes, that's a trademark) version of Trademarks-101!

Chapter 8

How Bulletproof Is Your Business?

There are several levels of trademark security for a business, ranging from neglect and danger to security and asset growth. I don't advise every business to aim for the highest level at the outset, but at least to learn the options and decide what really makes sense for a business of your size and circumstances.

Level I Trademark Manager:
The "Neglecter"

This guy takes no action of any type regarding trademarks. He does nothing. Spends nothing. Doesn't even give it a thought.

He picks brands simply because he likes them. He uses internet domain names because they seem good. Businesses at Level I generally don't last long. They're often headed for disaster, even if they have good products and are run by otherwise smart people.

Remember the case studies from the beginning of this section? Tales of companies with good products that were becoming successful, but failed to search their trademarks before they used them. One needed to change brands midstream, giving up valuable market recognition and good will. The other was bankrupted by the need to scrap their entire inventory, because it included an infringing trademark that should have been searched before using it.

<u>Who Should be at Level I:</u>

- Kids with lemonade stands.

- Sidewalk sellers of counterfeit handbags and wrist-watches.

- People willing to drop everything and walk away from their business efforts.

- Start-up businesses that haven't yet done any advertising, domain selection, brand selection, or manufacturing.

- And businesses that are going to graduate out of Level I, *tomorrow.*

<u>How to Graduate from Level I:</u>

Get *all* your existing Trademarks searched *now,* and *never* adopt a new trademark without first having it searched to make sure it doesn't infringe someone else's rights.

To get this critical clearance, hire a competent trademark attorney, find a trustworthy trademark search firm, or learn to competently search trademarks yourself.

To work with the trademark attorney, don't just tell them what you think the brand is. Have them look at your website, catalog, advertising, and the packaging, labels, and imprinting of every product you sell. While digital snapshots can be emailed, we need to see all the fine print on the labels. Or you can just send a box of actual products—especially if they're really cool and interesting—hint-hint! That's because you may be using more words or phrases as trademarks than you realize, which can create more opportunities for protection that can enhance your asset value.

Your attorney will conduct a basic search of the federal trademark database including registered, expired, and abandoned marks. Later chapters will explain more about how we determine whether there is trademark infringement, but I give my clients a conservative opinion about whether they're at risk.

If my client is at risk of infringing the rights of another trademark owner, I advise that they quietly select an alternate mark. They should stop investing in advertising the questionable mark immediately, and transition into the new trademark. That's much easier to do when they're doing it at their own pace and not after a complaint, under the requirements imposed by the lawyers for the big company that owns the trademark they are likely infringing.

You or your trademark attorney should also conduct an ordinary internet search (i.e. "Google") for each and every one of your brand names. That can help find trademark owners who are not in the searchable database. (What kind of fool would fail to register their trademarks to help others avoid infringement? Read on to learn about Level II)

Unregistered trademarks still do have some limited rights, and you can still face the dire consequences for infringing them, so be sure to Google all your brands, or ask your attorney to search them.

Alternative option 1: Hire your own searcher

Some attorneys don't do their own searching, and instead hire an outside search firm such as Thomson.com to conduct the search. You can hire the searcher yourself, but expect to pay several hundred dollars per trademark searched (about what your attorney would charge). Note that if you Google: "trademark search," you'll find dozens of companies advertising lower cost searches, but I don't advise trusting their work unless you've gotten a good recommendation from someone who can evaluate their results.

A reputable search firm won't be able to advise you on legal issues like whether your trademark infringes in a borderline case or how much you need to change your brand name to avoid infringement. I prefer having an ongoing relationship with my clients, and they seem to prefer that too, so your first choice is to find an attorney who will be part of your "team" for the long run.

Odds are, you'll have other questions and trademark needs over time, and you'll probably want the strategic guidance only someone who understands your business can provide.

Alternative option 2: Learn to do it yourself

This probably isn't attractive to a busy executive, but if you have a smart staffer interested in learning trademark searching (and even registration) techniques, it may be an option. This is most likely to appeal either to firms in the branding field (like advertising and marketing companies), or cash-poor startups and non-profits with a brand-intensive business like a catalog retailer with a wide range of their own product brand names. The only option for this, other than apprenticing with a trademark attorney, is the high-quality but somewhat pricey video course offered at LawyerlessTrademarks.com.

Preferred option 3:

If you're busy running your business, then outsource all these trademark responsibilities to an attorney who specializes in trademark law.

Level II Trademark Manager: "The Shoestring."

This guy makes sure all his trademarks are searched and safe, but he doesn't bother to register them. He has a relationship with a trademark attorney and invests at least a couple hundred dollars per year on trademark searches, probably more. He doesn't pick a new brand without first emailing the trademark attorney, asking for the usual quick search. Not all searches are equal, and none are perfect, but reducing the risk by 90% is still a smart idea.

The Shoestring isn't likely to go out of business because he stepped on someone else's toes. But he's much more likely to get his toes stepped on by a company that couldn't find his unregistered trademark when they were picking a new brand for themselves. He may face the cost of a lawsuit he can't afford (and which probably won't award him damages or reimburse attorney fees). Either that, or he'll just have to "shut up and take it" and let the big boys use his trademark because he can't enforce his own trademark rights against a trademark bully. This undermines his own rights, and devalues his business.

An earlier chapter revealed several stories that showed how those who failed to register missed out on the important advantages of registration:

My client that couldn't expand beyond a few states, because unregistered trademarks have only limited geographic scope, and someone else had gotten rights in the rest of the nation.

Another client that became embroiled in litigation because they failed to register a trademark. Their mark wasn't in the database when a competitor searched, so that led to a preventable lawsuit.

The client that litigated, but spent a lot more money and time on the lawsuit than needed, because litigating unregistered trademarks is more of an uphill battle.

Another client who got the short end of the stick in a negotiation over a trademark conflict, and had to settle for a far worse outcome than he would have if his trademark had been registered.

<u>Who Should be at Level II:</u>

- Businesses whose brands are not important or valuable and either don't use brands or can change brands without caring.

- Businesses with critical financial priorities that would kill the business if neglected. Feed your starving horse before buying fencing for a corral.

- Businesses who are at a pre-launch phase and can apply to register a mark at a later time.

<u>How to Graduate From Level II:</u>

Register at least your important trademarks. Certainly register your "house brand" (the company name that is on all your products—like "Ford") even if you can't yet afford to protect important product brands (like "Mustang" and "Taurus").

Prioritize your other brands, and register them as your funding permits. If it would be painful to have to drop a brand, or painful to see someone else infringing it, then register it.

Give your trademark attorney a chance to tell you what all your trademarks might actually be. He needs to see all your advertising material, website, product packaging and labels. I give serious prospective clients a preliminary analysis of their trademark portfolio as an investment in a long-term client relationship. I provide a list of their apparent trademarks, and advise them they should register all the valuable ones.

Caution: Beware the Dangers of Filing to Register Without First Searching

It can be dangerous to file to register trademarks that you haven't searched. This can be a real problem for those who proceed without a trademark attorney.

It happens far too often that a company that was going along just fine with their unregistered trademark hires an internet company to register their trademark (or does it themselves). Suddenly, that application turns into a lightning rod that attracts the attention of another company with a similar mark. Maybe the other company's mark is borderline dissimilar or the goods seem different. But it's close enough to get the other guys riled up and the legal machine steaming.

A conflict that never would have occurred becomes a real business headache. The mark you thought you were taking special steps to protect ends up being lost because you didn't search first.

Of course, if my client wanted to register a mark that might attract this kind of problem because a search found a conflict, I tell them either to think about phasing in a new mark, or at least to lay low, and cross your fingers that the other guys won't get wind of it.

Alternative option 1: Internet discount registrations

Beware of companies offering $199 trademark registrations. First, this doesn't include the Patent and Trademark Office filing fee (currently $275). Second, be wary about costs for the later steps for the application, so you aren't being drawn in by a low initial cost and later charged more than an attorney might for arguments and even routine paperwork. You won't get any associated searching or advice for the loss-leader fee. It's unlikely that the service will even be provided by a lawyer, and it may even be outsourced to overseas clerical staff. Ask yourself, what is my brand worth to do it right?

Alternative option 2: Learn to do it yourself

Again, this isn't attractive to a busy executive, but it may be an option for some others. Especially for low-budget brand-intensive companies. Some people manage to file their own without help at the uspto.gov website and not make serious errors. For those who like to have a good idea of what they are doing (like plumbing, it's not hard if you know what to do) the only comprehensive option I know of is the video course offered at LawyerlessTrademarks.com for a little less than a specialist lawyer would charge for a single trademark application filing. Of course, it requires many hours of study to master the skills.

Preferred option 3: The Bulletproof Trademark

For this, you hire the best trademark attorney you can, who gives you Bulletproof service to help keep you from letting trademark rights fall through the cracks. A Bulletproof trademark includes a search to make sure that you don't have a conflict, so your application doesn't become a lightning rod for lawsuits. Bulletproof service means you get the qualified legal answers you need to decide whether a trademark is safe and clear to use.

Level III Trademark Manager:
"The Adequate Executive"

This level includes some of my clients, typically the well-run smaller companies that have a more limited legal budget or who wrongly assume that trademark protection is a big-ticket item.

They register their company name and maybe several key product names. They usually have me do a trademark search on proposed new brands, but sometimes they forget.

The companies at this level often hear from me after I pick up their new catalog, and I ask them if they want to protect several new brands they didn't think to tell me about.

I often notice some glaring trademark usage errors in the catalog and send them back a marked up copy so they can avoid them next year. The errors may be using the marks inconsistently, not using the right symbol, and other serious errors that'll be discussed later in this book (and which can undermine or destroy your rights). You should at least know that proper trademark usage is *very important,* is cheap and easy to get right, and is very dangerous to get wrong. That's why this book has a whole chapter on the subject. It may be the most important section for many readers.

This level of client has done the basics, but doesn't worry much about trademarks or their importance to the value of his business. Without a good, proactive trademark attorney, he may risk dropping down a level. With a good one, he can effectively advance a level.

How to graduate from Level III:

Either find a good attorney who will be proactive and monitor your trademark needs, or have someone on your staff read this book and take charge of the issue internally. Probably a combination of both.

In any event, *someone* needs to be conducting at least an annual audit of all your trademark usage (before your annual catalog is printed), so you can make informed decisions about whether to protect your new trademarks. This must include a review of all your new product packaging or labeling.

And certainly, train all your key people (marketing, advertising, etc.) that you will *never* adopt a new brand name without first having it cleared by your trademark attorney. Never.

Level IV Trademark Manager:
"The Elite Executive"

This group represents my most successful clients. Maybe they don't like to spend more than needed for legal work, but they invest wisely in their trademark portfolio based on good advice.

The executive at the elite level knows that a trademark portfolio is a business asset that can represent real value when selling the business. He knows that advertising dollars aren't poured down a hole or used merely to generate current sales and profits. He thinks of advertising partly as a capital investment that builds the value of the brands it promotes. Your business stores that value in the trademark "bucket."

He has a policy in place in the employee manuals of key employees, and in the contracts with outside sources that ensures the following:

1. No new brand is *ever* adopted without clearance from the trademark attorney.

2. All new advertisements, marketing materials, and web designs are reviewed by the trademark attorney before being published.

3. All new brands are evaluated to weigh whether registration is justified.

4. Consider maintaining a "shelf" or inventory of a few likely future brands. Using an advanced "Intent-to-Use" strategy, these can be processed to approval by the Patent and Trademark Office and held "idling at the finish line" for several years at nominal cost, ready for immediate adoption. (More on this later where we discuss the Intent-to-Use application.)

The budget for all this depends mostly on the number of brands per year that need to be protected. For my major trademark clients, my charges for the annual reviewing of marketing materials and occasional clearance searches are relatively minimal and often included in the standard costs of registration. Ideally, there is a "trademark champion" in the company (who may or may not be the boss) who is educated about the issues and ensures that the plan is followed.

Who Should be at Level IV:

All businesses that care about enhancing asset value and aren't unusually cash-strapped.

How to Graduate from Level IV:

Graduation isn't necessary for most businesses, except that advanced asset protection strategies should be considered at Level VI.

Level V Trademark Manager:
"The Monster Brand Police Dogs"

This is a special level for businesses where the brand is the main asset. But there are lessons for Level IV executives here, too.

Examples include owners of famous brands like Coca-Cola, Microsoft, Starbucks and Chanel. Most of these examples sell products at prices greatly in excess of their generic competitors, based on the reputation of the brand. Other examples involve less famous brands, but where there is significant licensing or royalty revenue flowing from use of the brand.

In the firearms industry, we might include a company like RealTree, which licenses its camouflage technology to many manufacturers, along with permission to use registered trademarks like "Mossy Oak." There are a hundred other ways to camouflage a rifle, but the RealTree executives know that their brand is a valuable asset that justifies the massive promotional investment they make in it (which explains all those giant banners at the SHOT Show.)

The "Monster Brand" owners do more than just register their trademarks and sit back and wait. They police them. That means they specially arrange with a trademark lawyer or other agency to monitor all the trademark filings on a frequent and regular basis to see if anyone is applying for similar trademarks.

When something questionable turns up on the radar, their enforcers aggressively pursue the matter. Typically, they file an "objection" to the trademark application, which starts a mini-litigation in the Patent and Trademark Office over whether the application should be registered. That often scares off small applicants who often filed to register without first searching. They don't want to bother with the five-figure legal cost and prefer to surrender and pick another brand. The second prong of attack is a standard "cease and desist" letter that demands that regardless of the fate of the application for registration, they must stop using the mark or be sued.

This can be an aggressive, sometimes expensive strategy. But it makes sense to invest hundreds of thousands of dollars per year to protect a brand worth tens of millions. At a basic level, there are affordable options for monitoring your trademarks to help you learn as early as possible when a critical infringement occurs.

I remember 20 years ago working at a Seattle patent and trademark law firm that policed Microsoft's trademarks. I was the new guy, and was assigned the drudge work of sending dozens of these nasty letters to the multitude of companies that had adopted trademarks including the word "Micro". It seemed a little silly at the time, and some of the complaints may not quite have been justified, but in hindsight, it makes a lot of sense. Imagine if the software world were crowded with a lot of different "Micro-this" and "Micro-that" companies, and how that would diminish the importance of Bill Gates' multi-billion-dollar brand.

In the ammunition industry, if you want to see policing in action, try registering a trademark using the word "shock," and see how fast the lawyers for the Federal Cartridge Company (the Hyrda-Shok® bullet makers) come down on you.

How to Graduate from Level V:

Sell your company and its trademark assets for a hundred million dollars. Or at least graduate to Level VI in the meantime.

Level VI Trademark Manager:
"The Truly Bulletproof Firearms Business Owner"

The truly Bulletproof Firearms Business Owner may only be a millionaire, but he thinks like billionaires do, and employs their legal methods to preserve and protect the wealth he's created.

This guy has all his trademarks and patents in order, and is maximizing his business value. He probably isn't a "Level V Police Dog," but he's minimized the risk of distracting and expensive trademark lawsuits.

The Bulletproof level isn't about what trademarks and other intellectual property he owns. It's about *how* the property is preserved and secured.

The truly Bulletproof owner knows that you don't hold your intellectual property in the same corporation that makes and sells products, especially liability magnets like firearms technology. He has established a corporate structuring plan to preserve the "crown jewel" assets like patents, trademarks, equipment, and real estate in one or more separate holding companies.

Even if his manufacturing company gets sued when someone misuses his product, it has few assets, making it an unattractive lawsuit target. Even if the lawsuit bankrupts the manufacturing company (which has paid royalties and rent to the holding companies) the owner can start up a new manufacturing company, licensing the same patents and trademarks, and renting the same equipment in the same facility.

The Bulletproof owner also has plans in place to exit his business in style, without shutting down the business. He can transfer his business to the next generation or to key employees, and minimize the hefty tax bill.

He also has a plan in place to transfer the business to his heirs, without it being liquidated to pay estate taxes, and even protecting its assets from the lawsuits his kids may face and the ugly prospect that the business he built may be run into the ground by a squabbling partnership that could include his heirs' hostile ex-spouses, or worse.

He may even employ an aggressive strategy to pass on major corporate assets to the next generation, entirely exempt from estate taxes, by transferring patent and trademark assets when they are worth nearly nothing, and letting them grow in his children's trusts.

Challenge #1:

Very few lawyers are qualified to this kind of work, and most will say "it can't be done" (which is often true, in that it can't be done by them).

Challenge #2:

Some of these powerful methods need to be done at the early stages of a business, when the high cost for a top legal expert to implement a complex plan is prohibitive. Often, these powerful plans are implemented in a second business, when there are adequate funds and the wisdom to invest them.

How to reach Level VI:

See the entire third section on Asset Protection.

Chapter 9

How to Select Good Brands That Make Valuable Trademarks

Executive Summary:

- Every potential brand can be evaluated in multiple respects, including quality and strength as a trademark. You should work with your trademark attorney to *select only safe, strong trademarks*. Limit your choices only to the brand candidates that score high on the trademark scale, so that a successful brand can become a secure and valuable asset.

- Avoid brands that merely describe the goods, and *choose distinctive brands*, preferably ones that suggest a quality of the goods without describing it (like "Jaguar" suggests speed and beauty, without describing a car.)

- *Give your trademark attorney a quick chance to review your list of possible new brand ideas.* Without even searching for conflicts, he can quickly warn you off of any that will be difficult to protect.

Chapter 10

Picking Brands

Selecting new brands can be a fun, creative challenge. You can hire a branding consultant, or rely on your own instincts. But the key is to be sure that your selections are informed by an appreciation of what kinds of brands make strong valuable trademarks.

As a trademark attorney, I don't have any special training in branding, but I have enough experience over decades of practice to have some strong opinions. The important thing to recognize is that while a brand may be "good" or "bad" based on many factors, trademark issues account for some of those factors.

You can have a great brand that really sells, but it may be a lousy trademark that never becomes a valuable asset. If a trademark is like a bucket into which you pour your advertising investment and earned good will, this kind of a weak trademark is a rusty, leaky bucket.

Descriptive Marks – the Siren Song to Lazy Marketers

Trademark lawyers and marketers aren't always at odds, but in this case, we are. A lazy (or frugal) marketer wants to pick a brand that instantly tells the buyer what the product is or what it does. That can make the mark "descriptive" and can make it legally ineligible for protection.

Suppose a company has created a portable shooting rest for hikers to take into the back country. Like one of those cane-stools, but with a rest to steady your rifle or pistol. (If you find a way to make one of these practical, see me about a patent!)

A lazy marketer will be tempted to pick a brand that tells you just what it actually is, like "Shooter's Stool" or "Hunter's Seat." That means they don't need to work as hard to explain what the product is, because the brand already tells much of the story.

But I can't help them protect a brand name that merely describes a product. The trademark would be refused registration, and would not be enforceable in court. That's because every business has the right (and economic need) to be able to describe its products, how they work, and what benefits they provide. If we allowed descriptive brands to be tied up, then other businesses would not be able to tell consumers important information about the products they sell. That would be unacceptable in a healthy, competitive economy.

Worst case descriptive brands are ones like "Accurate" for rifles, or "Lethal" for ammunition. Every seller deserves the chance to explain that his products have these qualities, so it clearly would be wrong for one company to get protection for these words.

Sometimes, a client will face a competitor's trademark that seems descriptive to them (maybe to me, too) and wonder why I can't help them get "bad" trademarks like that. In reality, this is a judgment call by an individual trademark examiner, and sometimes descriptive marks wrongly get registered. That will tie my client's hands more than it should, and they have to work around the problem.

How do we deal with the rare descriptive mark? Take the example of the company that proudly owns a trademark registration of "Personal Defense" for ammunition. Now, we know that "personal defense" is a phrase commonly used by gun writers, defense trainers, and many other sources to describe the concept of self defense. A Google search would turn up thousands of items having nothing to do with the trademarked ammunition from that particular company.

There are several ways to deal with this problem when an examiner is too lenient in granting a registration to a descriptive mark. First, we can spot the problem when the application is pending and oppose the registration. If we miss that chance, we can file a "Cancellation" proceeding to cancel the registration. Or we can convince a judge that the mark is invalid when we are sued for infringing the mark. Some of those options can get awfully expensive. But what's more frustrating is finding that a descriptive-seeming mark has been registered for so long (over 10 years) that it has become legally "incontestable." Which basically means "forget it, and pick another phrase to explain the purpose of your own goods."

The flip side is that this benefit granted to long term trademark registrants means you have another advantage to registering your trademarks early. Once you pass the 10-year mark, you can stop worrying about challenges to your rights. If you can't beat 'em, join 'em.

Other marks may have seemed descriptive at first, but endured after the owners invested in them, and they gained "secondary meaning" in the minds of consumers. Examples are ones like: "National Broadcasting Company," "Global" van lines, and "Budget" car rental. In the end, a descriptive mark can take on force, but a trademark like "Avis" or "Hertz" will have much more legal strength right off the bat and less risk that it will fail ever to gain trademark status. Yes, people start restaurants with names like "Downtown Grill," and that can turn out fine in the end, but they face the real risk that a competitor has the right to open up next door with the same name, and exploit the customer confusion.

Suggestive Marks – Often the Ideal Choice

Suggestive marks are often the ideal, and are the ones that please both the marketing experts and the trademark lawyers.

A suggestive mark does not describe the goods (or services) but suggests desirable qualities of the goods. "Jaguar" does not in the least describe motor vehicles, nor would its use prevent any other automakers from describing all the qualities of their vehicles. But "Jaguar" conveys the image of sleekness, beauty, aggressiveness, and speed. This is a wonderful trademark of immense value as a corporate asset.

Of course, "Speedy" would be a lousy trademark for cars, because it is descriptive. "Speedwagon" was a trademark for cars, but that didn't grant the trademark owner Ransom Eli Olds ("R.E.O.") the right to prevent anyone else from using the term "speed" to describe their goods.

"Fast" for a drive-through burger chain is descriptive of the nature of service they promise, but "In-N-Out" suggests the same thing without actually describing it. Great trademark!

Amazon. That's another favorite of mine. When the online book seller first launched, many of us wondered what the heck a big river had to do with selling books. Of course, now that we know that Amazon sells *everything* under the sun, not just books, the image of a giant river makes perfect sense, suggesting immensity, dominance, transportation, flow. All the factors that fit perfectly with a retailing giant. It's easy to imagine the board meeting when they came up with the brand, and how it fit the spirit of their long-term corporate strategy.

Sometimes, a suggestive mark is so good, you almost think of it as being descriptive. Here's a way to test a brand for this. Consider the brand alone, and ask yourself if, hearing the brand alone, you'd have a good guess what the product might be. The word "Rebel" doesn't make you think of cameras, but it does suggest a lone, rugged photographer who travels to dangerous and exciting destinations (and also a free-thinking consumer who doesn't automatically pick Nikon).

The creative techniques used by branding experts are a great way to come up with good brands that suggest the qualities and benefits of your products.

A "Brandstorming" Exercise—How to Generate Good, "Suggestive" Brands That Are Legally Strong.

Let's try to come up with some good brand ideas for our hiker's portable shooting rest.

First, consider the actual qualities of the product itself:

> *Strong, light, portable, comfortable, economical . . .*

Then, consider the benefits the product gives:

> *Freedom, independence, accuracy, fun, sporting, humane to game, comfort, survival food, unspoiled scenery, unburdened game reserves, virgin, back country, conserving ammunition, keeping clothing clean and dry, useful for disabled or elderly, etc.*

What kinds of brand ideas can we get from these short lists (which could be much longer)? What words carry several of these meanings in the way that "Jaguar" suggests both speed and grace?

Ideas include names of famous people or groups who have these qualities like *"Davy Crockett," "Lewis and Clark," "Arapohoe."* That may face challenges to get the rights, but it helps us think of other ideas. Other people in general terms may be worthy: *"Mountain Man," "Backcountry Marksman."* We can consider associated geographic concepts *"Teton," "Treeline," "Trailside," "Echo."*

This is the kind of thing to get together with some key people in a relaxing environment and let the creativity flow, perhaps along with some adult beverages. Sometimes, constraining yourself actually opens up creativity, like in the games we played as kids on long car trips. (How many hunting terms can you come up with that begin with the letter "D"?)

Now, let's say you have a few good ideas that appeal. Maybe one of them is the term "trail." How would you like to see the list of all the trademarks that use the word "trail"? That's easy for your trademark attorney, who can give you a list of the words. Now, you may wonder why I would suggest you look at existing trademarks to make your selection, because anything you pick would infringe, right?

The answer is that first, most of the trademarks using "trail" aren't for hunting or recreational gear (though many will be). You may get a great brand inspiration from a granola brand, or footwear product. Also, the list will contain other brand elements to stimulate you. My quick search (it took me 30 seconds as I write this) turned up nearly 2000 "trail" marks. Some alive, some dead (another source of possibly usable trademarks). And that list (even just the first 250) gave me other ideas like *"tracker," "game," "hawk," "guide," "valley," "overland," "master," "ridge."*

One solid approach to creating a good trademark is to combine two words that create the overall impression you're looking to convey: *"Ridge Master," "Overland Guide," "Game Hawk,"* or *"Trail Tracker."* None of those are pure branding genius, but they're a lot better than some brands I see, probably won't face a descriptiveness rejection, and might even be as good as you might get for thousands of dollars from a mediocre branding consultant.

Here's what I did: I went to www.uspto.gov, clicked on "Trademarks" in the left column, then "Search TM Database (TESS)." I then clicked "New User Form Search (Basic)," and typed "trail" into the Search Term box and clicked the "Submit" button.

That gave me many pages of results to look over. Note that if you want to learn more about any listed trademark, you can click it and learn what goods and services it applies to. If it's something related at all to hiking or hunting, then you'd want to avoid it or at least get the advice of your trademark attorney to be sure.

Caution: If you're considering using this search technique to see whether a new mark infringes any other marks, beware. This simple search technique will miss many trademarks that your new brand might infringe. That includes marks that are similar but not identical, or that rhyme, or use alternate spellings, or a host of other reasons. That's why you want to have a searcher who uses advanced techniques to uncover these kinds of conflicts.

Anyone getting serious about mastering trademark searching should get thorough training, such as from the video course available at LawyerlessTrademarks.com.

But at least now you can see how trademark searching techniques can help your "brandstorming" creativity.

Arbitrary marks

Kodak. 325i. Model 70. Google.

These are trademarks that trademark lawyers love, but marketers sometimes don't. They are made up brands that have no meaning at all. That means the marketer starts from zero to explain the product. But at least it makes them unlikely to face a descriptiveness challenge, though they can still be rejected if they conflict with other marks – don't try to sell a car using the model number "325b."

But the marketers sometimes still appreciate arbitrary marks, because certain components still suggest certain desired qualities of the goods. Hard characters like "T" and "7" suggest to experts a more aggressive or masculine aspect (I'm serious). The sound made when saying the brand can be important (avoiding tongue twisters, of course). Even the fact that the brand is a short combination of numbers and letters suggests seriousness, like a German sedan, or a military rifle.

Made-up words can also effectively convey a desired impression. Drug companies do this well, with "Rogaine" suggesting regaining hair, "Viagra" suggesting vigor, "Motrin" suggesting painless freedom of movement. Internet, consulting and high-tech companies also seem to love this approach: "Accenture," "Aquantive," etc.

So give serious thought to picking and choosing characters, syllables, and word elements that have their own feeling or meaning that conveys the qualities of your products..

How Do You Decide What Is Your Actual Trademark?

This can be a challenge. Let's say you decided on "Trailside Rest" as the brand for the hiker's shooting rest and it cleared an infringement search conducted by your trademark attorney. The next question is, "What is the trademark?" Is it "Trailside Rest"? Is it "Trailside," with "Rest" being the description of the goods? That's something to weigh with your trademark attorney, in case either option gives you better protection, or reduces the risk of rejection or infringement. In the next chapter on trademark usage, we'll cover all about how trademarks are strictly followed by a "generic" term for the goods, like "Band-Aid® adhesive strips" or "Xerox® copiers," so we're considering treating "Rest" like that.

If you're going to create a whole family of products (let's say ammunition for hunters) using the word "African" in each brand (African Hollow Point, African Solid, African Big-Bore, African Upland) then you'll probably want to treat "African" as the brand.

But that doesn't mean you can't have it both ways. You can also treat the entire phrase as the mark, and register "African Big-Bore" as well. Registering "African" will protect you against anyone using that term as a trademark, even in combination with different words because they can't adopt the entirety of your mark. But suppose a competitor came out with "Austrian Big-Bore." "African" and "Austrian" might not be similar enough to be considered a case of infringement. But when you look at the whole of the marks "Austrian Big-Bore" and "African Big-Bore," you have a much stronger case.

Once you've decided which element or elements are your trademark, then you'll tell the world about your decision by placing the "TM" symbol right after the mark (you'll change it to "®" only after a registration is granted).

Chapter 11

Trademark Use and Misuse: Cheap and Easy to Get Right, Dangerous to Get Wrong

Executive summary:

- You can weaken or lose your trademark rights by using the trademark improperly. Trademarks must be used consistently, without modification, pluralization, or possessive-ization, and only as an "adjective" that describes a "noun."

- Great companies have lost great brands by allowing misuse, and smart companies work fiercely to make sure their valuable brands aren't misused by themselves or by others.

- To avoid misuse, always have marketing materials like catalogs and advertisements reviewed by a trademark attorney who can spot and correct the errors.

Proper trademark use isn't difficult or expensive, but misuse can lead to disaster.

Chapter 12

The Rules For Safely Using Trademarks

<u>Trademark Trivia Question:</u> What do the following things have in common: *zipper, aspirin, escalator?*

<u>Answer:</u> They all used to be trademarks. They each used to be brand names exclusively controlled by a company (Bayer sold Aspirin brand analgesic tablets). But over time, these brands became used generically (even by their owners) to describe the products they were associated with, regardless of the source.

That's a nice bit of trademark history, but there's an important question you should be asking yourself: *"How did these valuable brands become lost, and how can I avoid losing my own valuable brands?"*

The answer is in using the trademark properly, and not misusing it. This chapter will cover all the rules and pitfalls.

Rule #1: Trademarks are Always Adjectives

Let's go back to the parts of speech we learned in grammar school. Adjectives modify nouns, and usually an adjective comes right before a noun in a sentence.

<u>Adjective example:</u>

"The *green* ball's rubber core makes it bounce higher." (Green is the adjective, and it modifies ball.)

<u>Trademark example:</u>

"The *Spalding* ball's rubber core makes it bounce higher. (Now, the trademark "Spalding" is the adjective.)

All the other usage rules follow from this. If you follow this rule, you won't go wrong.

Rule #2: Never Make a Trademark Plural

This is a common mistake, but remember that only nouns are pluralized, and trademarks are never nouns. You would never pluralize an adjective, so it follows from Rule #1, that trademarks are never pluralized.

Misuse:

"You can use two or more Band-Aid*s* to protect larger scrapes." (If Johnson and Johnson had been sloppy about this over the generations, you can bet that "Band-Aid" would have gone the way of Zipper and Aspirin.)

Acceptable use:

"You can use two or more Band-Aid *bandages* to protect larger scrapes." (Here, the adjective trademark is properly followed by the generic noun, which is what takes the pluralization.)

Scrupulous use:

"You can use two or more Band-Aid® *brand bandages* to protect larger scrapes." (We've now included the "®" or "™" symbol, plus the purely optional "brand," which is used by companies worried about losing a valuable trademark to generic-ness.

Rule #3: Use the Trademark Symbols Properly

Marketers and advertising copywriters might not like the way the word "brand" breaks up the flow in the last example, and you don't always need to be this obsessive. Know the rules so you can know which ones you can bend. If your brand is one that's a "threatened species," like Band-Aid, which is often used by ordinary people as a generic noun, then your job is to be as scrupulous as possible at every turn. Of course, it's a marketer's dream to be the leading brand on everyone's lips, so this is a fine tightrope. You want to be the famous standard, but you don't want to get sloppy and lose everything.

The trademark symbol is good to include wherever practical, but also is not essential in absolutely every use.

The trademark symbol (whether "™" or "®") is most critical as applied to the goods or their labels or packaging. That's your actual trademark use that generated legal rights, and you don't want to make any errors.

In advertising and materials like catalogs, the symbol is important, but less critical. I advise that at least the one most prominent use of the trademark on a given catalog page should include the symbol. On the other hand, the symbol should *always* be used on every prominent placement of the trademark on the actual packaging or labeling for the product. In advertising copy and catalogs, you can relax a bit as needed to keep things practical and readable.

Which symbol to use? "™" vs. "®"? This is simple. Use "™" until a registration is granted, then you may use "®". If you use "®" unjustifiably, you may weaken any trademark rights due to this illegal misuse of the symbol. And because your actual trademark samples (packages, labels, etc.) are submitted to the Patent and Trademark Office to get a registration, you wouldn't want to embarrass yourself and face rejection for misuse by using the "®" symbol before it's time. The "™" symbol is just fine as a temporary measure. If you want, your fine print can indicate that a federal registration has been applied for, although that fact will be apparent to anyone searching the Patent and Trademark Office database.

Another question is where to put the symbol. It may be subscript, superscript, or whatever works typographically. It should immediately follow the last word of the trademark in text without a space, and there may be more than one symbol. For instance:

"African® Game-Gitter™ ammunition" shows that "African" is registered, and the three words "African Game-Gitter" (or the maybe just the last two—it's ambiguous) are considered as a trademark, but not yet registered.

And if you have a logo or design serving as a trademark, it should have the appropriate symbol, which may be right next to the logo or even embedded in it (such as reversed out of a block of printed color). If the logo includes words that are also your trademark, those words may also need the appropriate trademark symbol, in addition to the symbol for the logo. This can be optional depending on practical graphic limitations, but if one element is registered, I advise finding a way to legitimately use the "®" symbol in the appropriate location. Of course, for important decisions like this, run it past your trademark attorney.

Rule #4: Trademarks Should Not be Used as Nouns

You can be flexible on whether you always use "brand" or the trademark symbol in advertising copy, but you should never use the trademark in a sentence as a noun.

<u>Misuse:</u>

"A Remington is a good choice for most hunters."

<u>Acceptable use:</u>

"A Remington *rifle* is a good choice for most hunters."

<u>Scrupulous use:</u>

"A Remington® *brand rifle* is a good choice for most hunters."

Of course, some ads will just have the brand name alone at the top of an ad, like a headline. This is usually without the "generic" noun following, which is just fine. ("Porsche®—There is no substitute.") But as soon as you're putting your trademark in sentences, watch every use.

One good reason not to use a trademark as a noun is because it tempts you into dangerously modifying the trademark in ways you would normally modify nouns (like plurals and possessives).

Rule #5: Trademarks are Never Made Possessive.

<u>Misuse:</u>

"The new Mustang*'s* acceleration is improved over previous models."

<u>Acceptable use:</u>

"The new Mustang *model's* acceleration is improved over previous models."

<u>Alternate acceptable use</u> (avoiding the possessive issue):

"The new Mustang *model out-accelerates* previous models."

And I could see maybe breaking the noun rule and eliminating "model" if it were really important to your marketing experts, but this kind of delicate call should be run past a trademark attorney. In many companies, there are disagreements between the legal and marketing departments, and the executive has to make the final call.

There's another tricky factor. Your key trademark may also be your company name. Sometimes, you may be tempted to say something like "Ford's reputation for quality has endured for generations." Now, that isn't necessarily against the rules, because you aren't using Ford as a trademark on labeling of goods, but as a company name, which is a noun. So you can get away with that if you must.

But I still advise maintaining trademark discipline, and considering many attractive options:

"The Ford reputation for quality has endured for generations." (Now "Ford" is an adjective modifying the noun "reputation.")

"The Ford Motor Company's reputation for quality has endured for generations." ("Company" is the noun, and safely takes the possessive.)

Or in a case where the constraints of trademark rules force us toward a better result:

"At Ford, Quality is Job 1."

Interestingly, among its scores of trademark registrations relating to "Betty Crocker," General Mills has a registration of "Betty Crocker's" for cookbooks. Their marketing department must have decided that the book needed to have that personal-feeling title, so the lawyers registered the trademark exactly as it appeared, as an entirely separate mark from the standard ones without the possessive.

Rule #6: Trademarks are not used as verbs.

One way to lose trademark rights by becoming generic is to use the trademark as a verb.

Trademark misuse: "Just Google the address and you'll also get the telephone number."

Yes, I know everybody uses that trademark as a verb. It's become hip, and I'm sure the Google shareholders love the idea that their brand is so famous. But I guarantee that you'll never see anything published by Google with this kind of deadly misuse. (The Google in-house trademark attorneys are probably in a perpetual battle to do something about this "problem.")

One factor on the verb issue is that it also tempts you into modifying (conjugating) the "verb." Maybe GM could build a luxury SUV lifestyle ad campaign encouraging you to "Go Escalading" with your family. But that is a *new* and different trademark from the "Escalade" brand, and either should be avoided, or treated as a new mark given protection on its own merit.

Rule #7 Trademarks are not to be modified in any way.

This rule goes along with all the other grammar rules. Pick your trademark, and leave it alone. Don't think of your trademark as text that can be edited; think of it cast in stone.

Take the Crimson Trace Corporation, and their famous patented Lasergrips® pistol aiming accessories. Notice that their actual trademark ends in the letter "S." You or I might do it differently, but that was their choice. So they should use the trademark in that form, *never* shortening it to "Lasergrip." If they need to, they can say "A single Lasergrips® device costs less than a riflescope."

Nike would be in dangerous territory if they cleverly referred to the option of buying Adidas shoes as "Just Don't Do It." It would start suggesting that the powerful trademark slogan was just a sentence to be modified, and not a real trademark.

But that's my best advice to anyone tempted to modify any of their trademarks: "Just Don't Do It."

It's often tempting to modify ordinary trademarks when you display them different ways. For instance, say you own the trademarks "African Mag" and "American Mag" for ammunition. That's what is says on the boxes with the "®" symbol. But unfortunately, your catalog and ads are using all sorts of inappropriate variations: "African Magnum," "African and American Mag," etc. You don't change the trademark, for any reason. Just say "African Mag and American Mag."

Policing your own trademark usage.

Fortunately, sloppy trademark misuse by people outside your company isn't likely to kill your trademark, as long as you're scrupulous about your own usage. But some companies have made special efforts. Why else would the kid in the TV commercial sing: "I am stuck on Band-Aid brand 'cuz Band-Aid's stuck on me!" (Note that second "Band-Aid" is not possessive, but is safely just a contraction with "is," a relatively harmless noun usage protected by the first use of "brand.")

The most famous effort to protect an important brand from being lost because of generic usage is Xerox. Not only do they maintain brand discipline in their own use of the trademark, but they actively campaign to raise market awareness of their brand. You may have seen large print ads in the Wall Street Journal reminding you that "You can't xerox a xerox on a xerox." That sentence has the word "Xerox" used once as a verb, and twice as a noun. Three strikes. We can convert that to proper usage: "You can duplicate a document on a Xerox copier."

From the current Xerox Company website (I'm sure they won't mind my helping them spread the word):

> *"Xerox is a famous trademark and trade name. Xerox as a trademark is properly used only as a brand name to identify the company's products and services. The Xerox trademark should always be used as a proper adjective followed by the generic name of the product: e.g., Xerox printer. The Xerox trademark should never be used as a verb. The trade name Xerox is an abbreviation for the company's full legal name: Xerox Corporation."*

Chapter 13

Logos

One common question is whether to register your logo, or just the word trademark, or both.

The clear case is when you're a corporation that's paid hundreds of thousands for a big design firm to come up with a mysterious wordless shape that now symbolizes your company, like the ATT globe, or CBS eye. Of course you'll be registering that logo.

But the more common case is when a trademark has some design aspects to it, but also functions as a word alone. In almost every case, I advise registering the word mark as top priority, unless there is something very important about the design, and the logo is not expected ever to change over time, as graphic styles often do.

If in doubt, just ask yourself: "If someone started selling related products under a logo with a similar design, but with an entirely different word mark, would it really bother me?" If not, don't worry about registering the logo or design (you can still use the TM symbol and have limited common-law rights). But if it would bother you enough to have your lawyer intervene, then by all means apply to register the logo.

Here's why I advise registering both the logo and the word mark. Logos tend to be changed to keep up with styles of the times, and the word will remain constant. Imagine if you had secured a registration for a trademark that was borderline descriptive (like "Personal Defense" for ammunition) but only with the whole graphic design. If you ever significantly updated the design, then when renewal time came around you'd be unable to certify that the original registered design was still in use. You'd have to file a new application. Your old (incontestable) application would be expired, and your new design application would be open to challenge from competitors who think your mark is descriptive and should not be registered.

So be sure that important brands are registered as words, regardless of whether you wish to register the logo or design in addition. The "Betty Crocker" word trademark has been around for generations, but every decade or so they modernize Betty's image, and that image is then registered as a new logo trademark.

If you're still unsure about whether to register a logo, you can always defer the decision and rely on common law protection in the unregistered logo, with the full protection of the registered word mark.

Chapter 14

Working Effectively With Your Trademark Attorney

I enjoy working with clients on an ongoing basis, helping with their strategic big picture to build a valuable trademark portfolio. Here's how my clients and I work things out:

Initially, I may offer a serious prospective client a phone conference in which I give some strategic advice and a plan for securing their trademark rights. I may be looking at their web site, catalog, and the Patent and Trademark Office database in real time as we discuss their options.

Before we take any action, we formalize the legal representation with an "engagement letter" I send that explains all the details of representation including fees and legal uncertainties. I don't like anyone to be surprised down the road by disappointing results that occasionally can and do occur, so the letter (like this book) lays out a range of scenarios.

Once the engagement letter is signed, I can begin work, and be available for questions and legal advice as needed.

For a new client that's not a major publicly-traded company, I ask for a retainer that prepays the filing and legal fees for the project they wish me to work on. Usually, work can be completed in a matter of days or weeks, or whatever time frame is necessary. If any part of the prepayment is not used (such as if a trademark search shows bad news and a registration is therefore not pursued) it can be refunded or applied to other projects.

Information I Typically Need From my Clients to Get the Job Done Right

For a trademark search to determine if your proposed mark is safe to use, I need:

1. The mark, spelled exactly as it will be used (or the graphic image of the logo).

2. Any list of second choice marks. If the first is a no-go, I'll keep searching down the list until we get a "go," so you'll want to rank them in order of preference.

3. All the specific goods or services that the mark is (or will be) used on. Don't forget that a main trademark may end up being used on accessories, parts, cases, promotional shirts and hats, etc.

4. The time frame when use is expected to begin (or when use began). If there's a conflict or an infringement out there, I need to know whose use came first to determine whether you're in trouble with them, or if they're in trouble with you!

5. Any specific competitors whose rights you're most worried about infringing. If you have enemies eager to tangle with you, I should know so we can give them an appropriately wide berth.

6. Any other information about the importance of the trademark, other marks it may be used with, future expansion of use, or other factors in your business strategy that may relate to this.

To prepare and file an application for trademark registration, I typically need:

1. The mark, spelled and punctuated exactly as it will be used. If it's a logo or design, email a jpg graphic image file of the clean logo artwork—dimensions min 250 pixels, max 944 pixels. Also, for logos, let me know if you consider color to be an important part of the mark or not.

2. The legal name of the entity that will own the mark (see the Asset Protection section to help you decide this). This may be an individual, corporation, LLC, etc.

3. All the address and state of incorporation information for the owner entity.

4. All the specific goods or services that the mark is used on, or will be used on in the next year or so. Note that there is added cost for protection in multiple classes of goods. Guns, gun parts, ammo, etc. are all in a single class and can be covered with one filing fee. If you add in unrelated items like shirts and hats, this increases the cost.

5. If the mark is already in use, the date that you first began using the trademark (first sale, first sales website, etc.). If this was an in-state sale, I also need the first interstate sale or marketing effort. If you're unsure about dates, something like "at least as early as sometime in 2004" may be acceptable.

6. If the mark is already in use, I also need a sample (an emailed digital snapshot is typical) showing the mark as actually used on a label or package. Original graphic art source files are not acceptable for this proof of usage.

To advise on whether a case of infringement has arisen, whether you're the trademark owner or the accused infringer, I need:

1. Any legal correspondence you've received.
2. Information about the trademark that is accused of infringement (I can search to see if it is registered).
3. A sample or image of the goods and their packaging that is accused of infringement.
4. Any critical dates you're aware of, especially when use of either trademark began.
5. Any other related trademarks or information.

In many cases, I'll have other questions, but having the fundamentals in place at the outset will make the process speedier and more economical.

Chapter 15

Intellectual Property Overview

Now, let's leave the busy executives behind (You can jump to the Sections on Patents or Asset Protection). Let's dig deeper into the foundations and principles of trademarks. We'll also cover practical aspects of the registration process, so you can know what to expect in typical cases.

How are trademarks different from other types of Intellectual Property?

"Intellectual Property" is sometimes the most important factor in determining whether a business succeeds, and grows to the point of generating real wealth that endures over the generations.

Intellectual Property, or "IP," is a legal term for a category of property. It sounds like a fancy legal term, but it's really just a catch-all for property that isn't traditionally categorized.

Here's what IP isn't. It isn't "Real Property," which is what lawyers call real estate, including land and rights associated with land (like the right to stay in a hotel room at a time-share in Hawaii the third week in February each year). "Property" is all about rights, and whoever owns real property has the basic right to keep others away from the place he owns.

IP isn't "personal property," which is basically "stuff," like vehicles, machine tools and fruit salad. Owners of personal property have the right to keep their own stuff, so it can't be possessed or used by others without permission.

IP (Intellectual Property) rights also give the owners of Trademarks, Patents, and Copyrights certain rights over others.

Trademarks—Commercial Identifiers, Brand Protection

A trademark owner has the right to prevent others from using a similar brand name or logo on goods. This serves to protect his reputation and to prevent confusion in the minds of consumers about which company is the source of the goods. Trademarks are important to essentially every business and are therefore covered in great detail in this book.

The value of a trademark builds over time as a business develops a reputation for quality, and generates good will. Often, a trademark can be the most valuable asset of a business (consider Coca-Cola or Chanel.)

Patents—Technology Protection

A patent owner has the right to prevent others from making, using or selling his patented invention without his permission. Economically, that means that the patent owner can set pricing as high as he thinks the market will bear, instead of worrying about being undercut by competitors.

Patents are very important to technology companies, but in recent years they've become more important to businesses that aren't traditionally thought of as high-tech. That's because courts have expanded patents to cover innovative methods of doing business. Even low-tech business owners should at least read the intro to the Patent section of this book, if only to be sure you don't leave a patentable innovation unprotected just because you assumed it wasn't the kind of thing that patents protected.

Copyrights—Protection for Creative Works

A copyright owner has the right to prevent others from copying his "creation." That creation could be written text, coded software, a photo or drawing, sound recording, or any other creative work that is recorded in some way. That includes direct copies like photocopies and works that are based on an original, and works based on copyrighted works, without being a direct copy.

This book won't cover copyrights because there's little you need to know to protect these rights. Few businesses need to actually *do* anything to protect their copyrights. If someone copies material from your website or publications, you can call your lawyer to write a cease and desist letter, which is usually all that it takes.

Unlike trademarks and patents, copyright protection is usually automatic, free, and doesn't require any legal action or registration effort. Just create your work, and you own the rights. It's a good idea to use a standard copyright notice like "©2008 Arbogast Property Management LLC." That's not required, but it tells the world you intend to protect your rights.

Chapter 16

What is a Trademark?

A trademark can be a word, a set of words, a graphic logo, graphic type style, product shape, or slogan. A trademark can even be a color or a domain name.

Fundamentally, a trademark is an indicator of the source or the origin of goods or services. It's something that tells the public who's selling the goods, and it helps them know that it may be a quality or reputable seller, for instance. So when you buy a can of Coca-Cola, you know that it's made by not just anybody, or imported from China from a company using disreputable quality ingredients, but it's made by the Coca-Cola bottling company to their specific standards.

A trademark may be just a word: "Coca-Cola." No matter what the graphic design or image, the Coca-Cola Company still has rights in those words no matter how they are designed.

A trademark can also be a logo. One example of a logo used as a trademark is the red triangle used on Bass Ale. They've been using this symbol as a trademark for over 200 years (it was the first ever registered in Britain). It's a simple symbol without words, but is identified with that particular source of the goods. The CBS Television eye symbol is another example of such a symbol.

A trademark can be a graphic type style or design. Let's go back to Coca-Cola. They use their famous and distinctive cursive script on their soft drink packaging. Even if you used different words in that exact same script, and tried to sell soft drinks with it, you can bet that the Coca-Cola Company lawyers will be all over you—and that they would win the lawsuit against you, because you're infringing their trademark rights in that design.

The shape of a product can be a trademark. Another favorite example: Coca-Cola. The traditional hourglass shape bottle with the curves and ribs on it is very famously associated with Coca-Cola. Even if you used your own design of the label, your own word mark, such a use would still infringe their trademark rights. The L'eggs pantyhose egg packaging is another product shape trademark.

Slogans can apply as well. "Just Do It" is not the name of the product, and it's not the name of the company. But it's something that is used in conjunction with the sale of those goods and functions as a trademark. You can bet that slogan is all over Nike shoe boxes and clothing hang tags to make sure that they have used it with the goods, in order to get their trademark rights (because trademark rights require actual use of the mark on the goods, not just in advertising or catalogs).

Color is another example of a trademark. Take for example the "Pink Panther" insulation. The fact that certain insulation is colored pink indicates that it's produced by Owens Corning. No one else can make pink insulation because of the trademark rights in that color. John Deere green is another famous example of use of color as a mark. And those color cases tend to be pretty controversial and are rarely important for most businesses. Of course, color may be part of your trademark, but you aren't likely to be able to sue a competitor for selling a rifle that simply is the same unusual color as your rifle.

Functions of a Trademark

The key function of a trademark is to identify the source or the origin of goods or services. It's a useful consumer information tool. It tells buyers who's producing a product or service. Now that doesn't mean that when they first see the trademark that they necessarily know exactly which company is producing it. But the key is that it represents the growing reputation, the company goodwill. Over time, that trademark begins to gain meaning in the minds of the consumers. So by the time that happens you'd be very upset if anyone else tried to use a similar trademark to try to confuse customers into thinking that they were getting your product when really they were getting your competitor's product.

You Have to Use Your Trademark

There's one fundamental legal principle about trademarks that is going to underlie just about everything in the registration process, and that is that trademarks require actual use. To have trademark rights, you must actually use the trademark on goods or services in commerce. Simply conceiving the trademark, or simply planning to use it is not enough. Using the trademark is the only way that a brand can actually gain recognition in the minds of the consumers and thus earn trademark rights. And that recognition is what trademark law seeks to protect.

The registration process creates some streamlined approaches to simulate that recognition, but in fact you can't get a registration until after you've actually used the mark in commerce. So keep in mind that if you'll never use the trademark, you'll never earn the rights.

Who Gets Trademark Rights?

The first user earns the trademark rights.

Someone can plan to use the trademark, start sending out press releases about their intended use of the mark, and then get scooped (this does happen). A predator could actually start using the mark and gain the real trademark rights.

But there are ways that you avoid that by using certain Intent-to-Use registration procedures even before you start using a mark. Of course, those registration procedures let you gain tentative trademark rights, but you can't perfect those rights as an official registration until you've used the mark in commerce.

Unregistered Trademark Rights Are Geographically Limited

The question of who is the first user can be uncertain. Suppose we have one person opening a coffee shop in New York, and another person opening a coffee shop in California. They're both using the exact same trademark, and it doesn't matter whether they open their shops on the same day or years apart. If they're doing business in those regions, they each have trademark rights in their own areas. That's fine if all you're ever planning to do is have one coffee shop, but if you're planning to expand into a nationwide chain, you've got a problem. You have limited geographic rights if you don't register your mark.

Let's imagine the expansion scenario. Imagine that both of those coffee shops on the East and West coasts start expanding their businesses into neighboring states. And pretty soon, somewhere in the Midwest, they meet and find themselves opening coffee shops in the same state, in the same city, maybe next door. Now, there's a problem. Clearly, when that first shop opens up in Chicago, whoever opened it first is the first user and has the trademark rights in that region. This establishes the boundary line of the two territories.

On the Internet or in a mail order business, it's less of a concern. In that case, the moment you put up a website and start doing business on the Internet, you're using the trademark nationwide even if you haven't sold a product in every single state of the Union.

A Federal registration gives you the immense benefit of covering all parts of the nation even before you've started using the mark in commerce. And that's going to be the solution for our coffee shop owner. If you're the smart coffee shop owner, you'll get the Federal registration, and if someone opens up in New York the next day and is using the same name, they're in trouble, even though you've never done business in New York (or maybe anywhere, just yet.) You're the first user, and that application for registration means that Federal Trademark Law considers you to be the first user in every state in the Union, right now.

Chapter 17

Different Types of Trademarks

One type of trademark is a <u>trade name</u>, more commonly called a company name, or the "house brand." For example: the Ford Motor Company—Ford. When you buy a Ford car, you'll see the blue oval logo on it. The logo and the company name tell you specifically the name of the company that built and sold the car. That's a trademark that identifies the source of the goods. It's common sense that if you can afford to invest in only one trademark registration, make it the brand that appears on every one of your products, your company name.

A trademark can also be the <u>product name</u> or the model name, for instance: "Mustang." The Mustang brand is applied to the actual vehicle, and even if the vehicle lacked the Ford logo, it would still function fully to prevent infringers from using the word "Mustang" for automobiles.

<u>Service marks</u> are also trademarks, that cover services and not goods. McDonald's is a good example of a service mark. Even though you get physical goods in a bag when you use the McDonald's drive-through window, they're providing restaurant services in addition to providing edible goods under the trademark. Educational services, training services, and other such things are also common service marks. A consulting company would also operate under a service mark.

Other types of trademarks are less likely to apply to a typical firearms business, but they're worth covering.

<u>Trade dress</u> is a trademark concept that applies to the packaging appearance or to the look and feel of a product. Again, consider the recognizable Coke bottle or a Chanel perfume bottle. Even without any branding on it, the

packaging, the appearance, the shape, the look and the feel are distinctive enough that they have acquired the status of a trademark. They identify the source of the goods for the consumer.

Glock pistols were the subject of a trade dress dispute that was settled for an undisclosed sum when the Smith & Wesson Sigma pistol (still being sold) was believed to be so similar in appearance that consumers would be confused into thinking they were Glock products.

Another example of trademark usage that's unlikely to apply to most firearms businesses is the category of certification or collective marks. These are a special case. Examples include: Underwriters Laboratories and the Good Housekeeping Seal of Approval. Good Housekeeping is not manufacturing products or providing services (aside from their magazine), but the seal of approval is a different thing. That's something that's applied by other companies to their own products when Good Housekeeping certifies that it meets their quality standards.

Underwriters Laboratories certifies the electrical safety of products. Even though UL doesn't make products, they certify them for certain standards and qualities, and the manufacturers then pay a small fee to Underwriters Laboratories to use that certification mark on the product.

Look for "the union label" as another example of a certification mark. It certifies that a product was made by union labor. And this label cannot be used by other manu-facturers, unless they have the approval of the union that owns that collective mark.

Foreign Trademarks

U.S. trademark rights stop at the borders. If you need protection elsewhere, your trademark attorney can coordinate filings in other nations.

Generally, only big multinational companies with highly valuable brands like Coca-Cola and Nike end up worrying about foreign trademark rights. However, if you have some very specific foreign market that your product is going to be sold in, then you should consult your trademark attorney.

There are certain foreign benefits that you get by filing a U.S. application for registration. By filing in the U.S., you can get the benefit of what's called "priority" for filing a foreign application. "Priority" means that as long as you file your foreign application within a certain time after you file your U.S. application, it's treated in that foreign country as if you filed it at the time of your earlier U.S. application. That means you can worry less about a predator starting up ahead of you in the foreign country after he gets wind of your U.S. application.

Priority filing means that you don't have to hire lawyers to do everything all at once; you can get around to filing the foreign application a little bit later.

State Trademark Rights and Filings

In my 17 years of practice I have never once applied for a state trademark registration. They may still exist, but protecting your trademarks is a federal game for 99.9% of circumstances. Only in the rare instance that a local business would never conduct any interstate commerce would a federal registration be unavailable. The Federal process gives you that nationwide benefit the moment you file. In almost every case, you can simply ignore state trademark rights.

Chapter 18

Understanding Trademark Infringement

We could fill books of information and bookshelves of case law on what kinds of marks infringe and what kinds don't. As we've discussed before, trademark rights apply to similar marks. That means that a trademark doesn't need to be identical in order to infringe. That's because even similar marks can confuse consumers and lead to misunderstanding about the source or origin of the goods. The real question is: How similar is "similar"?

Word Trademark Conflicts

If you have two similar word trademarks, infringement can occur even if the logo or designs are entirely different. Conversely, similar graphics and similar logos can infringe, even if the words are different.

Two word marks need not be identical for infringement to occur. Different spellings don't prevent infringement. For example, if there is a registration for the mark "Quick-Glue" for a brand of adhesive, a mark for the same goods that was spelled "Kwik-Glue" or "Qwik-Glue" would infringe. The similarity of the appearance and spelling, and the similarity of the sound if the word were spoken out loud creates an infringement. So even a different-sounding word that looks the same, or a different-looking word that sounds the same can infringe.

Rhyming words can also infringe. That makes searching a challenge, but not impossible.

Another kind of relevant similarity is similarity in meaning. There are some words that may be of foreign origin that look different, sound different, and are spelled differently, but they mean the same thing or a related thing. Those sorts of words can create trademark infringement.

There are certainly no absolutes as to what infringes and what doesn't. But the more factors suggesting similarity, or confusion in the minds of consumers, the stronger a case for infringement can be made.

When we encounter borderline cases, whether evaluating search results or a potential case of infringement, we consider all these factors. Normally, I advise playing it conservative and advise against adopting a questionable mark. It's usually easier to find a different brand that has a clean bill of health.

Logo and Design Trademarks Conflicts

With logos and designs, similarity is in the eye of the beholder and mostly based on what elements are in the design. Logos and designs are more difficult to search than words, but there are ways to search for different aspects and elements of a design. When a trademark is registered that contains a design or a logo, all those elements are catalogued by a trademark examiner so that they can be searched.

For instance, let's say that your logo has a combination of arrows and horizontal lines and circles. Marks that are similar would all be indicated and listed in the Trademark Office catalog. If you were worried about infringing other marks that also have arrows in them, you would search for other marks that used arrows in the same class of goods.

I advise on each case individually and generally use a conservative gut feel to avoid future infringement risk.

Are The Marks for Related Goods and Services?

When considering whether a mark infringes another mark, another factor to consider is the relation between the goods and services offered by the two competing marks. In order to infringe, the goods and services for which the marks are being used don't need to be identical, but there is a higher likelihood of infringement if the goods and services being offered by the two marks are related.

One of the things we contemplate in this sort of infringement analysis are the trade channels. If a retailer sells one type of goods, it also may sell another related type of goods. For example, clothing and shoes might be considered related. Thus, a mark for footwear that is similar to a mark for clothing might cause confusion in the mind of the consumer about which company made the goods. When in doubt on this you should assume the worst if there's anything in your mind that says they might be related.

A company that has a broader range of products might have some crossover. For example, Nike sells both clothing and shoes. That's something that we need to consider.

We also look at the "zone of expansion." Would it be normal for a company using a certain mark for clothing to use the same mark for shoes? If so, it might be a logical zone of expansion for the company. For a business that sells only shoes right now, that may be all they've used their mark for, and that's all that they would appear to have the rights for. But if you pick the same mark or similar mark for clothing, that might not be a good idea. You could be vulnerable to a charge of trademark infringement if the other company expands into clothing. A court might rule that it was a natural zone of expansion of their business and that they have the right to that peripheral borderline area beyond what they're currently actually using the mark for.

For example, you're selling computer software, and someone is already using the chosen trademark for computer hardware or for computer consulting services. That's the kind of area where you need to be concerned about zone of expansion.

So, what kind of gut feel test do you use to determine if the goods are related? What I do is I just put myself in the shoes of the company that's using the other mark. When you do that in an emotionally detached way, and you're honest with yourself about what you might feel, you're going to do a lot better job of avoiding conflicts. Play it conservative when picking brands.

Even if it seems like I'm advising you to be a little bit too conservative with regard to avoiding infringement, it's still better to pick your third choice brand to use as the "bucket" to invest your business, marketing, and reputation value into, rather than picking a trademark infringement fight over your first-choice name.

Remember, the value of that trademark "bucket" is mostly in the contents (product quality, advertising investment) that accumulate over time. So, a third choice "bucket" that keeps you out of trouble is much better than a first choice bucket that you are forced to dump out because of an infringement lawsuit. That sort of thing can ruin a business.

Famous Marks

Famous trademarks are the exception to the rule that trademark rights apply only to related goods. We covered United Van Lines and United Airlines—just because they are both using the word "united" in their trademarks, the marks don't necessarily infringe, because they are for different goods and services, and they aren't within each other's zone of expansion.

Famous trademarks are the big ones that everybody knows, or at least everybody in a certain market knows. These are brands like Coca-Cola, Rolex, and Maybelline. There's no other company that sells Coca-Cola products unrelated to soft drinks. There's no company that sells Rolex mufflers or frozen foods. And there's no other company that sells Maybelline products.

These marks are all famous marks, and they have special rights that break the rule of related goods. The companies using these marks control the trademarks for the entire universe of goods because they have, over many, many years, and with immense investment, made those marks famous. The investment in the marketing didn't guarantee the mark's fame, but it was successful enough to result in the mark becoming famous.

When you hear the marks mentioned above, you know that there's only one company that uses that mark for all the goods in the world. Any use by someone else of that mark would tarnish the reputation of the company that created that mark.

So if someone opened a Rolex muffler shop, do you think that would tarnish the reputation of the watchmaker Rolex? Certainly no one would doubt that people seeing the Rolex muffler shop would see the name and instantly be thinking about luxury watches. This mental association with the name Rolex and luxury watches tells us that the muffler shop is sapping the Rolex reputation. It's actually using up the reputation of the original creator of the mark and the value of the original mark. In a generation, young watch buyers might avoid Rolex because it makes them think of rusty mufflers. Because it tarnishes the Rolex company's investment in their mark, we don't permit anyone to use that same mark for any other goods and services.

Some not-quite-scrupulous owners of certain trademarks try to take advantage of this principle when it's really not justified. Occasionally, a client of mine will receive a cease-and-desist letter complaining that my client's mark infringes someone else's trademark. An example—a mark like "Stealth" or "Terminator." These just aren't famous like Rolex or Maybelline, and you can easily imagine different companies owning them for differing unrelated goods (like United and United). However, there are certain seedy law firms or trademark owners that own these marks, and they're just in the business of sending out letters and trying to collect licensing fees.

These trademark owners argue that their mark is famous, and threaten litigation. But in fact, all they've done is accumulate a portfolio of trademark rights for different goods, as people have rolled over and paid them the royalty they're asking for! If you get one of those letters you *do* need to talk to a lawyer. It's not the end of the world. Sometimes you can works things out; sometimes these guys can be sent away with nothing. (Once, I almost had them getting ready to pay *my client* to use their mark!)

Asking for Trouble: a Clever Play on Another Trademark

Here's another rule of thumb. If you're picking a trademark, don't do what some foolish people do and get cute with someone else's trademark. If it makes people think of someone else's brand, you're asking for trouble! We've seen the newspaper articles about some sympathetic upstart who opens a coffee shop, and they've come up with a cute name that makes you think about Starbucks. They don't come right out and use Starbucks, but they get too "clever" with it.

One example is someone named Sam Buck. She opened her coffee shop and she called it "Sam Buck's Coffee Shop." Well, sorry Sam, it made us think of Starbucks. And we all know that you would have picked a different name for your shop if not for trying to grab some of the Starbucks recognition. Starbucks owns the rights, because they invested in the brand, creating its value.

Using Your Own Name as a Trademark

The fact is, you don't have the right to use your own name if it infringes someone else's trademark. There are plenty of other options for you.

This really bothers some people. People think they have the right to use their own name as a trademark, even if it infringes. But imagine the ridiculous result if that were an absolute right. For example, if I wanted to start up a car company I could find a friend named Robert Ford and make him a partner in the company. We could sell Ford automobiles under his name. People would end up confused, it would harm the Ford Motor Company, and it would all be a big sham anyway. Of course, you can use your own name just about any way you wish, *except* as a trademark for related goods of another trademark owner.

So if your trademark is a clever pun or play on another trademark out there, especially a famous trademark, let it go and do something else. Come up with your own really good quality brand.

Chapter 19

The Trouble with Searching Unregistered Trademarks

As explained earlier, common law trademarks are trademarks that are not registered with the Patent and Trademark Office. These are accorded minimal legal rights, but are better than nothing. Unregistered trademarks are hard to search and easily lead to lawsuits.

A common law mark can't be found in the Patent and Trademark Office (PTO) database, yet owners of these marks can have some rights. And even if that mark has been used only in one small part of the country, it has its rights there. But you're going to have a hard time expanding into all parts of the country if you're prohibited from doing business in certain states where someone else already has local rights to the trademark.

To pick good trademarks that don't infringe the rights of others, we need to be able to search "dead" marks that aren't registered, because these can may lead to owners who still have trademark rights, even though they failed to obtain or renew a registration. I should note that in the PTO search database, there are marks that are not registered but still listed, and that includes applications that failed to become registered and trademark registrations that became abandoned for failure to renew them when the owner stopped using the mark.

If a mark is "dead," that doesn't mean for certain that you can use it, because the owner may simply have forgotten to renew his trademark. He may actually still be using the mark, in which case you'd still have a problem. When I see a "dead" mark that looks like a concern, I don't stop there. I do a little more research.

I can often even track down the trademark owner, because their contact info is right there in the database. I might phone them up and ask them how I can buy an "Acme" brand lawn mower (or whatever pertinent product) from them. If the receptionist says, "Oh no, we don't sell those anymore," I make a note of it and my client is probably safe to use that mark. But if they say, "Hold on, let me put you in touch with our Sales Department," we might find that they're still marketing those goods even without a trademark registration, and I advise my client against using the mark.

But there's an even more effective way to find out whether a company is using a common law trademark. I do an ordinary internet search, using the Google search engine. I search for the company that I found in the trademark database and try to find out exactly what they're doing and what they're selling. It's very unlikely that their company's going to be selling goods under a certain brand, yet fail to have it anywhere on their website.

And don't forget that other companies may have cropped up using the same brand without registering it, so I also Google the mark itself, and not just the company name. You'd be surprised how useful that can be.

In some instances, my client will know about special industry publications and resources that might be useful to determine what trademarks are being used by people in their specific industry.

Chapter 20

Types of Trademark Applications

There are two types of trademark applications: Applications based on use, and applications based on an intent to use (ITU).

Applications Based on Use (the Trademark is Already in Use)

These are standard applications for when the trademark is already in use at the time the application is filed. They require the applicant to certify that the trademark is already in use at the time of application, and provide an example showing how the mark has been used. I file lots of these for new clients who've neglected their trademark portfolio, and are getting their trademarks squared away.

These are for playing "catch-up" and for registering marks that didn't seem important at first, but now clearly are.

Applications Based on Intent-to-Use (ITU)

The Intent-to-Use type of application is what I recommend for clients who have an organized trademark strategy. They will have me search the proposed brand, then if it is available, I'll file an Intent-to-Use (ITU) application even before my client starts using the mark or even announces their plans.

The ITU application secures your rights nationwide before anybody can even get wind of it. A business that's serious and organized about protecting its brands uses the ITU process. They often also register a domain name at the same time to prevent predators from grabbing the domain of newly filed trademark applications.

The ITU application does add a nominal ($100) fee before the registration is granted, because the certification and evidence of use comes at the end of the process, not with the application. That's done by filing a Statement of Use, after the application has been approved by the trademark examiner.

Advanced ITU Strategy

For the nominally increased fee for the Intent-to-Use process, it allows you some interesting and potentially powerful strategies. For instance, the process allows you to apply for several different trademarks that you might use later. You can see how they fare in the Trademark Office. If some of them are rejected, you can still use the others.

This process lets you accumulate a bank of examined trademarks that meet the legal qualifications to be a trademark, but that haven't yet been used. So if you're continually coming out with new products and product lines in a certain area, you can create a stable of examiner-approved brands that are registrable, because they've already gone through the entire trademark process. There were no objections from competitors, and the trademark examiner has given it the rubber stamp of legal approval but not yet registered it. And once they're in that phase, the moment you start using the mark you can file a Statement of Use, and then very shortly thereafter you get a registration.

In that situation, you get the added benefit of enhancing your own search efforts, because the trademark examiner does his own search. And of course, if one of those ITU applications acts like a lighting rod and attracts a complaint from a competitor, you can drop it without much pain, because you hadn't started using the mark.

You don't have forever to demonstrate use of the mark, after your ITU application is approved by the trademark examiner. You have six months from getting that stamp of approval to file your Statement of Use, and you can extend in six-month intervals for additional nominal fees. You can get up to 3 years of extensions, which can be worth much more to your company than the nominal fees you have to pay for the privilege of getting the extensions.

Chapter 21

Registering Your Trademark

The Registration Process

Most applications slide through the registration process fairly smoothly, and only a minority face some tougher rejections, sometimes which can't be overcome. But the vast majority of my clients' applications turn into granted registrations.

It takes roughly 1 to 1½ years to get a registration.

The first step is the filing of the trademark application. I file it online at the Patent and Trademark Office website, and immediately get a confirmation by email, which I forward to my client so they have confirmation of the filing. The confirmation includes the application's serial number, which will be used to track it until a registration is granted. Within a few days, the Patent and Trademark Office database will include the application, searchable by everyone with internet access.

The next step is that the Trademark examiner, a lawyer who works for the Patent and Trademark Office, is going to review your application just to make sure that it meets basic legal standards. Then, they'll conduct a search of the database and other records to determine whether your mark conflicts with any other marks. They're looking out for the other trademark owners out there, to make sure that an undeserved registration isn't granted.

Trademark Rejections

After examining the application, the examiner might respond with the good news that the mark has been examined and will go to the publication phase, which we'll cover in a moment.

Or the examiner might give you some form of a rejection. These days, that rejection arrives in my email inbox. A response is required within 6 months, or the application is abandoned.

The rejection is usually fairly clear and readable, with legal justification provided. Sometimes, there will be multiple reasons for a rejection.

Some of the rejections are easy to overcome. We might get a rejection that requires us to change the description of the goods, if the examiner considered it too broad, or misdescriptive.

The examiner may ask us to "disclaim" part of the mark. That's terminology that means that they believe that part of that mark is descriptive. Let's say you applied for "Dove Bar" for ice-cream. You may think of both words together as the whole mark. The examiner might say that you're required to disclaim the word 'bar' so that your rights don't extend beyond just the combination of words. Disclaimers aren't a big problem. It just means that the owner of "Dove Bar" won't have much luck suing the sellers of "Klondike Bar."

Other rejections can reject the specimen and ask for a substitute specimen if what you submitted is in some way inadequate in format or content.

The rejection may ask you to clarify if you're the common owner of a related conflicting mark, because you may have a family of marks that have a lot in common. Let's say you're in the restaurant business, and you have lots of different products you sell that start with the "Mc" letters, like McFish, McChicken and McNuggets. Now, that may be trademark infringement if those marks were being used by a different company, but the trademark examiner might want you to go on the record, saying: "Yes, this 'McDonald's Corporation' is us, and we know that these two trademarks appear to infringe." The Patent and Trademark Office just wants to get some kind of a reply that confirms that even though the two marks might be in conflict, it's okay because they're all owned by the same company.

A more ticklish, tricky and important rejection is that your mark is "merely descriptive." We covered that in terms of what makes a good quality mark; a mark that's descriptive is not entitled to protection. You can't trademark "fast" for cars or "refresh" for soft drinks because they describe the characteristics or benefits of the goods.

Let's say we face a descriptiveness rejection. You're not out of the race, but we have some work ahead of us. First, we can argue that it's not descriptive, but if that argument fails there's another good option.

The Supplemental Register – A Way to Bypass a Descriptiveness Rejection

The Supplemental Register is kind of a compromise solution to overcome a descriptiveness rejection. There is a process for transferring the application to the Supplemental Register, which has lower legal standards that allow even descriptive marks.

The Supplemental Register gets you into the same database as a normal trademark, it gets you listed as "Registered," and it lets you use the ® symbol. Thus, it gives you many of the benefits of a registered trademark. But it does not give you the legal rubber stamp of the examiner saying: "I'm unbiased, and I think this is a legitimate trademark." Instead, what the examiner says is: "I'm scratching my head over this, and I'm not sure if this is really a legitimate trademark. I'm going to leave this up to the test of time, or maybe a court to decide, should this ever be litigated."

The Supplemental Register is like a "sandbox" for questionable trademarks that really aren't ready for prime time, because we're not certain about them. After 5 years of use, we can reapply for registration on the Principal Register (the full-fledged standard register). Hopefully, in the 5 years of use, your mark has developed a secondary meaning, like National Broadcasting Company. But the Supplemental Register is a second choice; the Principal Register is really what we're shooting for in the long run.

When a mark is considered so generic (like "bullet" for ammunition) that it really doesn't distinguish the goods from others, then it will be ineligible for the Supplemental Register.

Rejections based on similarity to other marks

The Supplemental Register strategy doesn't help you avoid rejections that are based on a conflict with existing marks. The trademark examiner conducts a trademark search, and if they find that you're in conflict with someone else's trademark, they're not going to issue a Registration. And they're not going to let you transfer your application to the Supplemental Register. They're going to say: "Looks like your mark infringes someone else's rights, and I'm not going to do anything to facilitate that."

Now, the examiner is not going to contact the other mark owners and tell them that you're thinking about stepping on their trademark rights. The examiner is not going to take any affirmative steps against you. They're just going to keep rejecting your application.

Publication and Opposition

Let's say you've overcome any rejections and passed the examiner's hurdle. The next step is that your application is "published for opposition." This gives the public, including some other trademark attorney policing a competitor's trademarks, a chance to weigh in and try to persuade the Patent and Trademark Office that there is a real conflict they might not have considered.

Here's what happens in an "opposition proceeding": Essentially, the opposer writes in to the Trademark Office, to tell them that they think that if your trademark were registered, it would infringe their trademark rights. There's a two-month period for the competitors to do that, and you just get to sit and wait and wonder whether this target out there has anyone shooting at it.

In fact, the process is more formal, like a mini-litigation, and can easily cost five-figures for each side. Usually, it leads to a negotiation between the parties. An applicant may drop the application and pick another brand, or take a license and pay royalties, or persuade the opposer that they are wrong. Or, they argue against the opposition.

Of course, you don't want to find out about a conflict when someone has opposed your mark. You want to find out about it before you've even applied for a registration by doing a good trademark search, so your application doesn't become a lightning rod that attracts opposition and litigation.

There's another process that's a lot like an opposition, called a "Cancellation." Oppositions apply to pending applications. Cancellations apply to granted registrations. If you discover a registration that should never have issued, you can pursue a cancellation proceeding, which is another mini-litigation in the Patent and Trademark Office.

Allowance

Assuming that you dodged the opposition bullet, the next step is that we get a Notice of Allowance telling you that your trademark registration has been granted. At least, for applications based on use.

If we filed an Intent-to-Use application, we have one more step. Remember that the Patent and Trademark Office doesn't grant registrations on marks that aren't yet in use. So we need to file a statement of use to demonstrate the actual use. That's when you'll include the specimen (a digital image of the actual label or package showing use of the mark) and certify the date of first use. If you haven't yet used the mark, you have 6 months to file the statement of use. That can be extended by 6-month periods for up to a total of three years.

With an Intent-to-Use application, sometimes, my client starts using the mark even before getting through all the approval process. In that case, we can file an "Amendment to Allege Use" at any time, to get that step out of the way. That basically puts your ducks in a row, so that later when the processes are complete, you'll get a registration instead of a Notice of Allowability.

The Importance of Honesty in the Trademark Process

Sometimes my clients ask me if they can get some advantage by fudging on some of the application information. It can be tempting to fudge the date of first use or even whether the mark really is in use. It's tempting to avoid those extra Intent-to-Use fees and just say that the mark is in use. So you wonder why not claim a phony use. Or sell one product to your brother-in-law, and then say that the trademark is now in use in interstate commerce when in fact you're really not in business yet and your product is not ready to sell yet?

Bad idea. Not just because it's morally wrong, but because in litigation, everything like that always comes out. All of the little fudges are inevitably revealed in the courtroom or by all the reams of discovered documents, and when they are revealed it's going to look bad for you. The jury is going to think of you as dishonest on all accounts. Odds are you'll have invested in a major brand and you're going to lose the brand, you're going to lose the litigation, and you're going to lose the investment in the litigation cost. You just don't want to go there. Also, don't expect an employee to lie under oath to help you win a trademark lawsuit. So, honesty pays in the long run.

If you're worried about having the rights in the mark when you're in the application process, then it's better not to try to register it, and try to get away with using your mark if you're worried about attracting unwanted attention. But best of all, just pick another brand that you can really invest in, really fill that bucket with value and make it an asset for your business.

Post Registration: Continuous Use is Required

Trademark rights exist only as long as there is actual continuous use of the trademark. That means even if your registration still shows up as "live" in the Trademark Office website when you do your periodic searches, but you stopped using it a year and a half ago, you don't have trademark rights, and you wouldn't be able to sue anyone for infringement.

It may look like a registered mark, and your competitors may think it's a legitimate trademark, but your trademark rights aren't enforceable unless you're using the trademark.

You could try to sue a competitor for infringement, but you'd lose because they could quickly prove that the mark was no longer in use. A mark can be abandoned even though the registration is still in the PTO database.

"Continuous use" does not mean that you're selling at least one product every day, or that your restaurant remains open 24 hours a day. Continuous use just means that you're continuing to use the mark in your business. For instance, we know that "Olympic" is a trademark for athletic entertainment sports contests that happen every 4 years or so. That's considered "continuous use." "SHOT Show" is a trademark of the NSSF, even though that mark isn't used on trade show services for most of the year.

Use your common sense on this, but the point is if you shut down the part of your website that sells that product for a year because you don't feel like selling it anymore, or if you're not sure you're going to continue selling that product, you've probably stopped using it and your trademark may no longer be valid.

Trademark Renewal

Instead of issuing registrations that last forever and leaving us to wonder from an issued registration whether the mark is still in use, the Trademark Office has a procedure for renewal so that after a period of years, trademark owners are forced to renew the mark. Unrenewed marks become abandoned for all to see. Renewal is a simple process of certifying in your filing that it is still in use and showing evidence of the use, just like we did with your original application.

There are several steps that occur over the life of a trademark registration, but in simple terms, they are renewals at 5, 10, 20, 30 years and every decade thereafter.

Chapter 22

Domain Names

Why You Should Probably Grab a Bunch

I advise my clients to take domain names seriously. They may have a website with one domain, and be happy. That's usually a bad idea. I suggest grabbing every related domain name you can. If you have acme.com, get acmeinc.com, acmefirearms.com (if that's your product line,) and even acmesucks.com (seriously).

It's not so much about what you are going to do with the domains, it's about what others can do with the domains. It may be a disgruntled consumer who posts his tale of woe on his acmesucks.com website. Or, it may be the "gnats" who try to earn a few pennies a day from each site, trying to get ad revenue for clicks from people who were looking for your site. If they get diverted, you may lose sales.

And you should register every one of your product brand names as a domain, if possible. Of course, if your product is the Eagle™ brand spittoon, don't expect to find eagle.com available to register. But if your brand is more distinct, you'll probably be able to register a domain like "trailsidetracker.com."

If you have a web staffer with advanced internet skills and an advanced web advertising strategy (like Google Adwords), you can use those tools to determine what the popular searches are, and try to get domains that match what consumers are searching. That kind of research can even help you with a more effective brand selection strategy.

The domain world is filled with predators and oppor-tunists. The moment you start using a mark (or your application is available in the database) others are going to see it, and maybe grab the domains before you do. There are certain legal limitations on what the opportunists can do, but it's usually expensive to restore your rights. It's much easier is to spend $7 a year on each domain you want to keep others away from.

If a profitable mid-sized business with multiple products doesn't have 50–500 domain names, they probably are leaving themselves open to problems.

And in my opinion, just focus on the "dot-com" domains. Maybe grab the ".net" and others for your one crown jewel company brand name. But "dot-com" will always be the "beachfront property" for internet business, in my opinion. Better a mediocre "dot-com" than a great "dot-info" or "dot-biz." There are significant resources out there that advise what tends to make domain names more or less valuable. (i.e. Shorter is better than longer, avoid hyphens, etc.)

One caution: At the time of this writing, certain domain registrars (such as Network Solutions) were engaging in some sneaky and dishonest tactics. When you inquire at their website whether your desired domain name is available, they essentially say "no, but we'll sell it to you for triple the normal registration price."

They use your query at their website to find out that someone is interested in the name. Then instead of letting you buy it at their site, Network Solutions grabs the domain name for themselves, and then offers to sell it to you at an inflated price. Then, if you go to a different domain registrar (like GoDaddy.com, which is an honest one) your inquiry will show that the name is "taken."

Lesson: don't trust Network Solutions.

How are Domains and Trademarks Related?

Remember the principle that trademark rights apply only to related goods or services? There can be several identical trademarks peacefully coexisting. But there can only be one domain name owner.

That means that you can have rights in a trademark, but not rights to the domain name (united.com is owned by the airline, not the moving company). And someone else could have rights to the domain name when you, as the trademark owner (like United Van Lines), don't. But you can always get a different domain name that solves your problem (unitedinc.com, unitedusa.com, unitedvanlines.com, etc.).

Sometimes, a domain name is actually used as a trademark; for instance, in online retail services. "Amazon" is a trademark that is not only applied to the boxes in which they deliver the goods, but it's applied to the website and it's applied as the domain on the website. Just like the "Home Depot" sign outside the big warehouse store, the "Amazon" name displayed up in the browser line may be considered a trademark.

If Amazon had been foolish enough not to have captured that website "amazon.com," and you grabbed it and tried to use it to sell books, they'd be all over you, because that's trademark infringement. In fact, even if you came up with a website that was available, let's say "amazon123.com," sold books on that website, that's trademark infringement too, because you are using that word as a brand in conjunction with your goods, and that creates confusion.

Domain Name Recovery

You can also use your trademark rights to recover domains from "cyber-squatters" who grab domains that others obviously have legitimate trademark rights in, hoping for an extortionist's payoff.

That doesn't mean you can go out and take back just any domain that you think would be best for your business. This is true even if the domain owner has bought the domain as an investment, and holds it as a part of their portfolio of domains when they're not really using it.

But there's a special case for "cyber-squatters," a procedure by which a trademark owner can go after someone who's clearly reserved a domain name because they're trying to take advantage of the trademark owner, and trying to extort money from the trademark owner.

This procedure is much cheaper than a trademark litigation. It's a relatively low-cost (4–5 figures) bureaucratic process in which you merely need to show evidence that the cyber-squatter picked the domain because it relates to your particular goods and services. They picked it after you started using your trademark.

The domain recovery process is often suitable when my client is a relatively well-known company, and we find that someone registered the plural version of my client's trademark, for instance, because they want to get some traffic from misspellings.

We can sometimes get them to cough up the domain by paying a fairly tolerable price that's in the couple thousand dollar range, instead of pursuing the recovery procedure. Yes, that means paying off the bad guy, but the goal is to get you your rights as cheaply as possible.

In some cases, we can also get some advantage from my client's trademark rights if the cyber-squatter has "parked" the domain in a certain improper manner. We look at the site that displays on our browser when we enter the domain name. To earn a few cents per day to pay for the cost of holding the domain, the owner sets up a site that looks like a search site, with choices that often relate to commonly searched terms, and especially things related to the domain.

For instance, if a squatter grabbed the misspelled "remimgton.com" there might be links on the web page to gun retailers, with labels like "buy Remington Rifles." That's not just cyber-squatting, it's trademark infringement, because they're selling related goods using the trademark or a similar mark.

Which means that the teenage entrepreneur in Rio Linda who grabbed the domain is going to swallow hard and act fast when he gets a serious demand letter from a trademark attorney.

Of course, he can always simply park their domain in a place that doesn't forward to these competing sales. If it's just parked saying, "This domain is available for sale," then you don't have a trademark case against them even if you do have a cyber-squatter case against them.

Section II: PATENTS

Chapter 23

What I Wish Every Business Owner Knew About Patents:

1. *Never* assume a valuable innovation is "unpatentable." If you think it's *new*, and it's *valuable*, STOP RIGHT THERE. Contact a patent attorney for a qualified opinion of whether it's patentable. You'll often be surprised what is.

2. *Keep good records* of your technology development. Proof of the date of invention is critical to patent rights, because patents go only to "the first to invent." Without proof, you can lose your patent rights in a dispute.

3. *Know the deadline to file a patent application.* You have only one year from the first public or marketing activity to file the application. Miss the deadline, and your rights are lost forever.

Chapter 24

You Think You're Not a High-Tech Business?
READ THIS STORY ANYWAY!

Fatal Assumption #1:
"Oh, It's Probably Not Patentable"

Once upon a time, everyone thought that only hard technology was patentable. Machines, chemicals, circuits. You couldn't patent software, you couldn't patent methods of doing business. That doesn't mean there wasn't real innovation going on in those areas, but everyone assumed they were legally unpatentable.

In 1979, Dan Bricklin invented the first interactive spreadsheet software, VisiCalc. It was a revolution that allowed ordinary users to use that now-familiar grid of boxes to process and organize their data, so that changing one number would then change all the calculations automatically. The concept has since been adopted in programs like Excel, Quicken and a host of other commonplace applications.

Imagine the value of all the spreadsheet software sold in the 1980s and 1990s. Which explains why Dan Bricklin is a now household name, famed for his 400-foot yachts, and his enormous charitable foundation.

No? You never heard of Dan? That's because Dan took some bad advice back in 1979. Dan listened to someone who told him "you can't patent that kind of invention." Dan never got the patent. He made no attempt to patent one of the most important software inventions of the information age. No patent. No yacht. No billions.

So even if you're not in high-tech, remember Dan Bricklin, who should have been a billionaire.

Fatal Assumption #2:
"Oh, It's Not Big Enough to Be Patentable"

What shape are the buttons on your cell phone or PDA? Are they round, flat, or concave? Who cares?

Well, one company cares. 3Com, the company that makes Palm Pilots (you know, they have a removable stylus that lets you write on the screen) cares plenty.

A guy who works at 3Com had a habit of using the point of his stylus to press the little buttons on his PDA. The problem is, his stylus slipped off those hard plastic buttons, because the designers made them dome shaped for people's fingertips.

One day, the frustrated guy had the magic moment of invention, took the device apart, and turned the buttons over so they were concave. His stylus never slipped off again.

So he told the patent department at 3Com about it.

How do you think they reacted?

First, let me tell you how my brilliant co-author reacted. She's been married to a patent attorney for a dozen years, and hears about this stuff over the dinner table all the time. "You can't patent that!" she said.

Wrong, honey.

The patent department at 3Com saw a good thing right away, and invested in getting the patent. Now, that patent probably won't affect 3Com stock much, but the reality is that any competitor with a stylus device (including things other than handheld phones and PDAs, I'd guess) will be disadvantaged in the marketplace.

I can imagine the product reviews: "The Sony Device is excellent, but users who punch the buttons with their stylus will probably prefer the Palm." No one will ever know how many sales were shifted because no one dropped the ball on the path to the patent goal line.

The inventor didn't drop the ball. He didn't ask whether it was patentable. He took action simply because he thought it was a nifty idea.

The patent department didn't drop the ball. They knew that small ideas can still be patentable. Little improvements can be valuable.

Like the feature that takes ordinary windshield wipers and has them wipe only intermittently, for light rain. Small idea, right?

The inventor was awarded tens of million of dollars from automakers who infringed his patent.

Would you buy a car without intermittent wipers?

How to Determine if Your Innovation is Patentable

All you need to ask yourself are two simple questions: "Is it new?" And: "Is it valuable?"

"Is it new?" just means that you didn't copy it somewhere else. Don't worry yet about a patent search, or how much it differs from what is "old." Only that you (or your employees) were the first to come up with this concept.

"Is it valuable?" means that *if* there were a way to protect this concept for yourself, you'd have a significant economic advantage over your competitors.

But *don't* ask "Is it patentable?" That's your patent attorney's job. And let me say that you may get different opinions from different patent attorneys. Some will be too conservative and say "no" when they should dig deeper and find a "maybe." A few may be too gung-ho, or even unethical, and say "yes" when there's no hope, and they just want your money. What you need is a "Goldilocks" patent attorney, who will be smart and creative in looking for an "angle" for real patentability, but honest about the actual uncertainties and risks, so you can make a well-informed business decision about the investment.

The kinds of "low-tech" inventions that most people wrongly assume are unpatentable include internet business methods like the concept of "one-click" ordering from websites. Less controversial concepts include manufacturing sequences, work-flow processes, financial processes, and a host of others. I like to tell my clients that, "if your janitor comes up with a *valuable new* way to mop the floor, then it may be patentable!" (Note that I used the words "new" and "valuable" in that example.)

"The Inventor Modesty Trap"

Even high-tech inventors can underestimate patentability. There are lots of myths like: "You can't patent a firearms cartridge" flying around out there that have since been disproved (by your author, in fact).

But in my practice, the greatest barrier to patent rights is "The Inventor Modesty Trap." (Business owners and managers: If you have technology employees, have them read this section.)

The Inventor Modesty Trap occurs when a smart, creative inventor comes up with something in the ordinary course of his work that's actually a valuable innovation, but it doesn't even cross his mind to ask about patenting it.

You see, he feels like it was easy to invent. Not a big deal. Just part of his job. It just "came to him." He thinks that patentable inventions are supposed to be hard work, so his invention must not be patentable. But what he has forgotten is that it is actually his job to invent things and to develop new products or to solve technology problems.

I wish I could post a sign on the wall of every shop, every lab, and every engineering cubicle of all of my clients saying:

Got a new idea?

Could it be valuable or important to the company?

Then call the patent attorney!

At this point, if any low-tech business owners are convinced that their company will never generate a valuable innovation, they may skip all the rest of the following patent chapters, and turn directly to the Asset Protection section.

Chapter 25

What inventions are patentable?

How different does an invention have to be to be patentable? Everyone knows that a major new product that is entirely new is patentable. But what about improvements and incremental changes? The answer is that there is no limit or lower threshold for patentability. But if a small improvement is new and valuable, then that improvement can be patentable.

For technology companies like those in the firearms industry, the usual question is whether a minor (but new and valuable) improvement can be patentable. The answer is YES. There is no prohibition on patenting small improvements that meet the normal requirements for patentability.

You can't patent a car, which has already been invented. You can't patent a heated steering wheel (though one prospective client thought he'd invented this in the early 1990s before they were common—a quick patent search helped him avoid a pointless investment in the cost of a patent application).

Perhaps you could patent a steering wheel heater with a new sensor function that concentrates the heat where the driver grips it. If that feature provided valuable advantages, then it may be patentable. But only that feature would be patented, and competitors could always use heated steering wheels without the feature.

Small inventions earn small patents. But small patents can still be valuable.

Not All Patentable Inventions Are Worth Patenting

The fact is that most of my clients pursue patent protection for only a minority of their patentable inventions. Only the valuable inventions justify the investment in the patent process. That's a common sense business decision. There may be a new invention every day that actually could earn patent protection, but few of them would provide any economic advantage over competitors, who could solve the problem a different way, without using the invention.

On the other hand, strong patents are tough to get around. Try designing financial computing software without a spreadsheet grid having certain cells displaying a value that is a mathematic function of the numbers in other cells. If the key feature is patented, then you either pay a royalty, or don't bother competing.

Chapter 26

Why Everyone Wants Patents

A Patent Provides Potent Pricing Power

Patents are a substantial economic investment, but can provide immense value. Smart technology companies invest in patents not because they want more plaques on the walls, but because they want more *profit*.

A patent owner enjoys the power to set the price of the patented product based on what he thinks the market will bear. He doesn't have to worry about being undercut by low cost, low-quality competitors. Pricing is based on product value, not manufacturing cost. That can provide profound profits.

It's all up to the patent owner. A patent can mean that yours is the only product on the market with the key patented feature. That can mean improved profit and market share. Or, it can mean that your competitors may agree to license the patent on your "take-it-or-leave-it" terms, and pay you a reasonable royalty to be able to use the patented feature.

It's funny, but I have lots of savvy clients who aren't exactly in love with patents. They know that they aren't cheap to acquire, and they can be incredibly expensive to enforce in court (more on that later). Some business owners have told me: "You can get around any patent, so why bother?" Or that they had a bad experience trying to enforce a patent, and will never do it again. They are sour on patents.

Then, I get the call. It turns out that they've just developed a new invention that they're sure will be extremely valuable and profitable. When that happens, all the costs and downsides go out the window, because the idea of being able to sell a valuable product without price competition is too important to ignore.

Here's what I often advise a client who decides not to invest in patent protection on minor products and features: "Don't worry, when you come up with an invention that's worth patenting, you'll probably find yourself awake at 3AM some night with a knot in your gut telling you this is the one to patent."

For a good example of a patent providing potent pricing power, consider the patent owned by the Crimson Trace Corporation (a client). It protects the concept of a grip for a pistol, with a laser on the upper part of the grip. When someone tells me that you can get around any patent, I ask them why we never see $50 knock-offs of this product at gun shows. The only products of this type are sold by the patent owner, and they command hundreds of dollars, based on the owner's assessment of the product value and market demand.

One dream patent scenario: IPO, buyout

One of my clients lived the dream. Back in the dot-com boom, a small company that was a big player in internet advertising invested heavily in patent applications for all their new ways of doing advertising business on the Internet. (I learned all about "cookies" and how they preserve your privacy while knowing everything about you!) As they had hoped, they had a successful IPO. It was my first client I ever followed as they went public.

What amazed me most about the IPO was the Yahoo! Finance news blurb about the IPO. It was only two sentences. It named a few executives and mentioned the stock price in one sentence. The second sentence? It told how many patent applications they had pending!

That told me that Wall Street thinks patents are awfully important. It maybe even overestimates the value of patent applications, because they need to be granted as patents before they give real legal value. But I learned that for many clients, patents are a great asset to an investor or a buyer, because they mean you have *something* to sell that can keep the business profitable.

Postscript: Not only did this company survive the dot-com bust, but in 2007 it was acquired by Microsoft for $6 billion. The company parking lot should be brimming with Ferraris by now.

How a U.S. Patent Can Provide Market Power in Other Nations

Of course, U.S. patent rights are legally limited only to the United States (we'll talk about foreign patents later). There's no legal effect on someone who knocks off your product in China, sells it in Germany, to a customer who uses it in England. But most of my clients are happy with a U.S. patent, because it protects the U.S. market from imports and domestic knock-offs.

And in many cases, a U.S. patent can essentially still secure worldwide market power. Again, consider Crimson Trace's "Lasergrips®" products. They have a great patent that has long prevented competitors and knock-offs from installing a laser into the grip of a handgun. Which is why they command top dollar in the U.S. market. Yet they also sell large contract quantities to foreign police and military agencies in other nations, at good prices.

So why aren't competitors undercutting them on those foreign sales? Surely, a Chinese company could copy the product and sell it for half of what my client does. But there are other factors at work. First, foreign customers still want "the best." And Crimson Trace used their patent to dominate the U.S. market, which is the most important in the world, especially for firearms. That earned them world-wide recognition as "the best."

Another factor that gives a U.S. patent power beyond our shores is that foreign predators sometimes won't even bother with knock-offs when they're excluded from the U.S. market. It might not be worth the investment, and they may just pick another target.

Even responsible multinational companies might respect your patent overseas, because they'd rather have a single product they can sell worldwide, instead of one version without the patented feature for the U.S., and another version for the rest of the world.

Patents Aren't Forever

It used to be that patents expired 17 years after they were granted. Now, it's 20 years from the filing date, which is not much different in the end. After a patent expires, it's over. Anyone can copy the invention disclosed in the patent without risk. In fact, all the expired patents out there represent "safe havens" for any company to copy.

That's part of the philosophy of patent rights that inspired the Founders to put patent rights in the U.S. Constitution. The idea was (and is) that inventors get a temporary monopoly on their invention, backed up by the courts, and in exchange, the nation received a detailed disclosure of how the invention worked and was made. That increases the free flow of technology information, which is good for the economy and was arguably a factor in helping the U.S. to become the dominant world economic power.

Trivia Factoid: Until the Bill of Rights was ratified, the only mention of "rights" in the U.S. Constitution was in conjunction with patent rights.

Chapter 27

The True Meaning of "Patent Pending"

Not only does a patent have no legal power after it's expired, but it's important to realize that a patent has no legal power before it's been granted. A filed or "pending" patent application provides many benefits, but enforceability is not one of them.

Simply filing a patent application gives some important benefits:

- It lets you use the words "Patent Pending" on products and marketing materials, which tells the world you're doing everything you can to lock them out. That alone may be enough to scare off some competitors in borderline situations, especially when tooling or marketing costs are substantial.

- It proves your date of invention at least as of the filing date. Hopefully, you have better records going farther back, but at least it's indisputable that you invented it by the filing date.

- It means you "beat the clock" and preserved your patent rights by not waiting for more than a year after public activity to file it.

- It secures the right to file foreign applications, giving you a year to decide whether to invest in foreign patents and in which nations.

But a pending patent application does not give you any enforceable rights. Many of my clients have told me how frustrated this makes them, having already invested in the patent application, seeing their product knocked off, and not being able to do anything about it. Here's what I tell them that usually makes them feel better:

First, it's a darn good thing that you can't sue before a patent issues. Imagine if everyone could. Not every patent application deserves to become a patent, so we wouldn't want others tying up your legitimate business on a "patent wish" that has no hopes of coming true. And even if they get a patent, it might end up not being as broad in scope as they hoped, and might not cover your product. So it's a good thing we don't allow patent lawsuits until a patent examiner has determined that a patent is really justified.

Second, when my client complains about having to wait to sue until a patent issues, I remind them that their competitor is helping them "make their market." True, the competitor gets to keep all the profits during the year or two before the patent issues, but that usually isn't much, given the investment in marketing a new product. And the marketing investment by my client's competitor ends up benefiting my client when the patent finally issues, because it raised overall awareness of the product category. The competitor is "making your market."

Occasionally, one of my clients will say that all they really want is just to be able to say "Patent Pending." I caution them that it's a big investment, and the competitors might still not give them much respect, unless a patent actually issues. Sometimes, if that's all they really want, we can file a "design patent" application, which does little more than protect the ornamental appearance of a product (like the shape of a lamp base, for instance). Because design patent applications require very little lawyer brainpower or time, they are a small fraction of the cost of a "utility" (regular) patent application. It's a cheap way to buy the right to use "Patent Pending," if you're really not looking for legal rights in the long run.

I should also note that some companies out there use the phrase "Patent Pending" when they haven't filed a patent application. That's improper, but there is little others can do about it.

I also find it amusing and pointless when companies proudly imprint their products with the numbers of patents that have been expired for generations.

Why Design Patents Are Critical to Firearms Businesses

Let me tell you a serious story about how one small gun company could have prevented the big boys from copying his best product.

At the 2008 SHOT Show, I wandered by the Kel-Tec booth on the second day of the show, and stopped to say hi to the owner. I asked him how the Show was going. "Not very good. Have you seen the cover of today's *SHOT Show Daily*?" He showed me a picture of what looks like his P3AT or P32 pocket pistol.

Here's why George was so down in the dumps (actually, one industry observer described him as "madder than hell.") The pistol on the front page wasn't his, it was Ruger's. George's niche market is now going to be shared by a 500-pound gorilla. I didn't do any detailed research beyond checking out the nice pistol at the Ruger booth, but we can bet that Ruger hasn't done anything legally wrong here.

The problem is that Kel-Tec didn't have any patent protection on their hot little pocket pistols. And they easily could have. George certainly knows they should have.

Of course, you can't patent just anything, because even a new pistol might not have any truly patentable innovations. But there's one type of patent that's easy to get, and perfect for situations where you want to prevent a competitor from producing a very similar-looking product. It's called a design patent.

Design patents simply protect the appearance of a product. In this case, a design patent probably would have protected Kel-Tec against such a similar looking product. The investment is only a fraction of what a typical utility patent costs, and would force a competitor to design a product with a different appearance. That won't keep them from competing, but it makes them work a little harder.

That's why I advise that every important new pistol, rifle, stock, or other product with a distinctive appearance be considered for design patent protection. A couple thou–sand dollars is cheap compared to the cost of product development, and it's nothing compared to the price of needlessly letting a competitor freely copy the appearance of your product.

Chapter 28

If You Don't Document Your Invention, You Risk Losing Your Patent Rights

The U.S. grants patent rights only to "the first to invent." Even if another person later comes up with the same invention, and files a patent application first, the first *inventor* is the only one entitled to the patent. There's no race to file the application like there is in some countries, and like some propose for the U.S.

But if it turns out that an issued patent was granted to someone other than the first inventor, the patent is then invalidated. (It's not transferred over to the true inventor.)

If there are two people who claim to have invented the same thing (and each filed his own patent application), the legal question is, "Who invented it first?" And in the real world, that'll be answered by a judge or jury who hears all the evidence. So the inventor should make a habit of creating the kind of evidence that will be believed later (remember, we're talking about creating *real* evidence, not fabricating it later.)

The typical standard evidence for invention date is an "Invention Disclosure" document (which can be informal) that illustrates and explains all the novel aspects of the invention. That document must be signed and dated by the inventor or inventors, and signed and dated by two witnesses who have read and understood the document. If the invention date is ever disputed, the inventor and witnesses can testify credibly about the invention date. In large technology companies, engineers and scientists are provided with forms to disclose their occasional inventions and have them reviewed by a patent committee that decides which inventions are worth patenting.

Your patent attorney can provide a suitable disclosure form that leads the inventors to generate a legally sound disclosure, and one which helps management to assess the value of the invention.

One weakness of a conventional Invention Disclosure is that it could be created fraudulently after the fact. Or worse, a jury is wrongly convinced that your dated disclosure was fraudulently post dated.

The best way to avoid this risk is to use an ongoing inventor's notebook (like a lab notebook with a sewn binding and page numbers) that shows the evolution and progression of the concept, with each pertinent page signed and witnessed. That would be much harder for a jury to imagine is fabricated, especially when it fits with all the other evidence like emails and calls to suppliers, fabrication of prototypes, and the like. A sewn-binding "Composition Notebook" from Wal-Mart is much better than loose-leaf notes.

Incidentally, it is a myth that a sealed registered letter is adequate proof of invention. Yes, one could be presented as evidence, and unsealed in court, but it is nowhere near as persuasive as a inventor's notebook that shows the progression and evolution of the idea.

It doesn't hurt also to fax your patent attorney a copy of the critical documents, so that there's a back-up with his date stamp. In addition, good documentation helps your patent attorney to better understand the invention, and to advise you and prepare a patent application much more effectively.

Chapter 29

The Missed Patent Filing Deadline That Will Kill the Million-Dollar Invention

Many clients have hired me to patent their *second* invention. Why not their first invention? Because by the time they called me, I had to break the tragic news that it was too late and that their first invention could no longer be protected. You see, they'd been marketing their products for more than a year when they called me. Their rights were forever lost because you have only *one year* from the time the invention is made public or marketed to file a U.S. patent application.

There's always some legal uncertainty about exactly what activity will start this deadline clock ticking. If there's any doubt, consult a patent attorney well before the earliest possible deadline to be certain about when your patent application must be filed. And even if you think that your past activity would never be found out, a patent litigator will tell you that a determined defendant will seemingly *always* find out the secret in their investigation.

So don't avoid telling your patent attorney about borderline activity just because that's what he wants to hear. You don't want to spend thousands getting a patent, and a small fortune on patent litigation, to have it all later invalidated. Keep inventing, and patent the next invention in time.

But while the one-year filing deadline is absolute and unforgiving, it presents a valuable opportunity to spend up to a year aggressively testing, marketing and selling an invention, to learn more about its commercial prospects before deciding whether to invest in the patent process. You may find out that it's not worth investing in a patent, or you may refine the invention or come up with something even better to patent.

The best way my clients avoid losing patent rights unintentionally is to contact me while the invention is still secret. When they tell me about their marketing timetable, I can advise which activity will trigger the one-year deadline. I calendar the deadline, and give my clients a reminder of when it is time to start an application or let the invention go into the public domain, where anyone will be able to copy it.

Chapter 30

Secrecy

You're Not Paranoid
If They Really *Are* Out to Get You
(But They Probably Aren't)

A word about secrecy. It's important, but don't obsess about it. The reality is that few if any businesses are actively trying to steal anyone's inventions. And if you keep your invention secret, you probably aren't marketing it very well.

The sensible and conservative approach is to keep your invention a secret until a patent application is filed. But to get to that point, you need to have tested and verified the invention, which probably means trusting your suppliers and other businesses you need to work with.

To state the obvious, avoid working with anyone who is truly untrustworthy and unscrupulous. When you work with good people, the key is that they *know* that you want the invention kept secret. Tell them that if they reveal the information, it can kill your patent rights, killing the project. There's nothing wrong with a formal non-disclosure agreement, but the point is to prevent the disclosure in the first place, not to sue somebody later for being loose-lipped.

Once your patent is on file, it's probably safe to tell the world, unless you have special strategic issues.

Be aware that the patent applications are normally published 18 months after filing. If you don't plan on getting foreign patents, you can ask that the application not be published. You may have special security reasons for this, so be sure to ask your patent attorney to request this before the application is filed.

One good reason not to let an application be published is because you're trying to patent a secret process. Say you have a way of manufacturing ammunition that produces more accurate ammo in half the time. Perhaps there's no way to reverse engineer the process by looking at the end product, so you don't give away the secret by selling products profitably. In that case, you might want to do without the patent altogether, and just keep it secret (like the Coca-Cola formula). But you might decide that a limited 20-year patent monopoly on the process is better than the risk that the secret might get out, leaving you with nothing. In that case, you don't want the application published. That's because if you fail to get good patent protection you'd rather fall back on the trade secret, without letting your competitors know your secret.

Chapter 31

Why Some Companies Hate Patents

The reason some companies hate patents goes beyond the disadvantages they suffer when their competitors get good patents that put them at a disadvantage.

The first reason is cost. Patents are a major investment. They require many hours of time by a specialist to prepare and file the application, then hours more to argue in response to rejections.

The application is usually the bulk of the cost. At present rates, that can be $5000–$20,000. The rest of the process to get a patent when things proceed typically can add another $5000–$10,000. Fortunately, the upper end of that range is very rare, especially for the kinds of patents my firearms industry clients need.

But what the patent-haters hate most is the idea of having to go to court to enforce their patent. That can easily cost hundreds of thousands of dollars. Some small companies know they could never fund that kind of litigation, so why bother even getting a patent you would never enforce?

Why Smart Companies Invest in Patents

With the immense cost of enforcement, why do so many well-managed and profitable companies invest in patents? Granted, the big companies can afford to bankroll lawsuits, but that doesn't explain why smaller companies pursue patent protection for their important inventions.

I advise my clients who are worried about investing in a patent they could never afford to litigate that a patent is like a pistol on your belt. For it to protect you against crime, it would rarely, if ever, need to be drawn, because the muggers would see it and leave you alone. And if the mugger persisted, drawing the pistol and pointing it at him would cause him most likely to back away. Shooting the mugger would rarely, if ever, be needed. (In some jurisdictions, shooting a mugger might lead to legal bills that could rival patent litigation!)

Similarly, simply owning the patent puts your competitors on notice, and most companies don't want to get tangled up in your patent rights. Contrary to popular belief, the biggest companies are most likely to be respectful of your patent rights. If a competitor does infringe your patent, usually "drawing the gun" (having your lawyer send them a cease-and-desist letter) causes them to back down. Only in the rarest case is the expensive lawsuit needed, and these generally are pursued only when the value flowing from the patent serves to fund the litigation. If the patent is adding a million a year to your bottom line, you won't hesitate to litigate it.

Chapter 32

Understanding and Interpreting Patents

The Anatomy of a Patent

Patents and patent applications are divided into several sections, each with a specific purpose. Knowing how they work is helpful to understanding issued patents. It's also important when reviewing a draft of a patent application your patent attorney is asking you to review and sign under oath.

The first major section of a patent is the "Background," which tells the story of the problems faced in the technology before this invention came along to solve them. It usually makes the most interesting reading. It's the one part the inventor can proudly show to his spouse or parents, and they may have some hope of understanding why his invention is important. It's also the section that leads my clients most often to say: "Wow! You really understand the invention! I couldn't have written this better myself." The Background is helpful in the future to help a judge and jury appreciate the invention, but it's really more marketing than legal force.

The "Detailed Description" (some of the section names vary depending on the attorney) is usually the longest section and contains all the details of how the invention is made, how it works, and all the possible variations that are imagined. It usually discusses the patent drawings, using part numbers that identify components in the drawings. When I write a Detailed Description, I do it as if I'm writing very detailed "captions" for each of the patent drawings.

This is a critically important part of the patent application, because it's the foundation for any patent protection. For it to be protected, it must be illustrated and described. And after the application is filed, this part can't be changed, so I always include as much detail as possible, giving us the chance to protect one of those details we might not have realized was important.

The Drawings are essential to illustrate the invention. I usually ask my client for certain views that I think best illustrate the invention, and they provide them in CAD form, which saves some cost on the formal drawings. But I can also work from crude sketches if that's what we have. The Patent and Trademark Office has strict and arcane rules about drawing details, which makes it just about impossible for your ordinary good technical drawings to meet standards.

The "Claims" are where the rubber meets the road, legally speaking. They're the numbered paragraphs at the end. Each sets out in precise and sometimes arcane form exactly what the invention is. Some people say that reading patent claims is like eating sawdust without butter. A little dry.

Claims are sort of like the wording on a deed that sets out the boundary of a plot of land ("Proceed 150 feet North from post A, then 200 feet east...") A patent may have one or more claims. A typical application has twenty claims, because that's how many the Patent and Trademark Office will let us include without paying extra fees.

Some claims, including the first one, are written like a separate paragraph and are called "Independent Claims." These are usually the broadest and most important claims. Many of the other claims refer back to another claim and add a particular feature or limitation to the claim ("The tricycle of claim 1, wherein the seat is mounted rearward of the front wheel"). This is just a shorthand convenience to make it more apparent what the key feature of the claim is, without having to write out and read through all the rest of the claim language. But an independent claim can be individually infringed and enforced.

Chapter 33

Patent Infringement and Claim Interpretation

Some people think that you can get around any patent if you have a clever lawyer. Speaking as a "clever lawyer," I can assure you that this isn't necessarily true, certainly not in many cases. Some patents are solidly written, with a broad scope of protection that can't be gotten around. Others are written more narrowly, whether because the lawyer failed to see an opportunity for protection, or possibly because broad protection wasn't deserved.

I sometimes assist my clients in "designing around" a competitor's patent, whether because they were accused of infringement, or because they want to be sure a new product doesn't cause legal trouble. As an engineer by training and a firearms technology expert, I can analyze the competitor's patent and advise which features or characteristics of their product they must change to be sure it doesn't infringe the patent. If the patent is narrow, my client may still have a solid product. If the patent is broad, then they may be out of luck.

When a client calls me to ask whether they infringe a competitor's patent they're worried about, I look at the patent claims, and compare them with my client's product. If the product has each and every feature listed in any one of the claims, then it infringes that claim. It doesn't matter whether it infringes one claim or all of them—it's still patent infringement. It works the same way when we're looking at whether a product infringes one of my client's patents.

What You Can Learn From a Lousy Patent

Here's a simple patent claim:

> *1. A child's self-propelled vehicle comprising:*
> *a frame;*
> *a seat connected to the frame;*
> *a front wheel assembly pivotally connected to the frame*
> *and including a front wheel;*
> *the front wheel assembly including a steering handle*
> *operable to pivot the assembly;*
> *a pair of pedals operably engaged to the front wheel;*
> *a pair of rear wheels connected the frame; and*
> *a noise making device having a first portion operable*
> *to selectably engage at least one of the wheels to generate*
> *noise, and having a second portion connected to the handle,*
> *and having a control element to control whether the noise*
> *maker engages the wheel.*

So, I've invented a tricycle with a noisemaker that can be used like a bell or horn, by engaging the wheels like a baseball card.

Now, let's design around this claim, which is actually a good example of a poorly-drafted claim. It has lots of faults that will render it almost valueless.

First, the claim doesn't cover seatless scooters that use the concept of a controllable noise maker using wheel engagement.

Second, it doesn't cover vehicles with rear steering instead of front steering.

Third, it doesn't cover pedal-less vehicles, whether motorized or having other propulsion (like a scooter).

Fourth, it doesn't cover vehicles having only one rear wheel (like bicycles).

And it doesn't cover systems where the noise controller switch is mounted anywhere other than the handlebars.

A claim that looked good at first glance is revealed to be a pretty bad claim that fails to cover all the potentially useful applications of the innovative concept. That's why claim drafting strategy is by far the most important expertise I offer as a patent attorney.

So all I need to do to help my client design around this claim is to help them find one feature that they can do without, and still have a good product. There's also a lesson here that when a patent application is written without care and attention to the business needs of the patent owner, the patent may be nearly worthless. It pays to have a patent attorney who understands your business.

Sometimes, when I've written a patent application, and my client's reviewing it, they're concerned that we didn't make all the claims broad enough. First, I often explain that the main description portion of the application should be as detailed as possible, because more detail in that portion does not narrow the protection. But in the claims, I create a range of claims with different strategies. Some will be much broader, some narrower. This provides insurance in the event that one of our broad claims turns out later to have been too broad, leading it to be rejected by an examiner, or invalidated by a court. Then, we'll still have backup claims that may still provide meaningful protection.

And when infringement of my client's patent is in question, I look at the questionable competing product, and determine whether it infringes any of the claims, using all of the principles above.

Chapter 34

Enforcing Patent Rights, Even Against Import Knockoffs

Sometimes, they say that a patent is "just a ticket to court." And no one really wants to be in court. But we've already covered why patents are so desirable and valuable, which is why so many smart businesses buy that "ticket."

Usually, a patent dispute will be resolved without litigation, when the infringer realizes that he will likely lose. Only rarely does the case need to go to court.

One concern of many patent owners is what to do when it's hard to find the infringer. Import knock-offs are the big worry. But they needn't be. Even a Chinese-made knockoff imported by a fly-by-night company can be easy to stop. Here's the trick: don't worry about going after the manufacturer or importer, just go after the seller.

It's quite common for a client to tell me that they hate seeing the knock-offs on the shelves of Wal-Mart or in Cabela's catalog, but have no idea who the producer is. I tell them not to worry. Usually, a brief letter to the retailer, along with a copy of the patent, is all it takes to get the products pulled from the shelves, and an apology. Those big companies have no desire to get tangled up in a losing patent litigation over a low-margin product that is only a tiny part of their business. Problem solved.

And if you know when imported knockoffs are coming into the U.S., you can let the U.S. Customs Service do your enforcement work. They have the power to stop any import they believe infringes a U.S. patent, and it's a lot cheaper than funding a patent infringement lawsuit.

Enforcement isn't always a breeze, but the rule of thumb is that a patent will deter many infringers from even attempting the infringement. The threat of a patent lawsuit will cause most infringers to stop. And there are often realistic ways to enforce your patent even when the manufacturer is hard to identify.

Chapter 35

Patent Searching

A patent search can save my clients big bucks. Like the old client of mine years ago who really thought he'd invented the heated steering wheel. Of course, patent attorneys don't necessarily have any special knowledge about what's been invented and what hasn't. We have to research to find out.

But my gut said that heated steering wheels had already been invented even though I'd never seen one at the time back around 1990. So I did a quick search on the Patent and Trademark Office database. Today, you could Google "heated steering wheel" and get close to a million hits.

Of course, I found dozens of patents on the subject, most owned by various big automakers. They covered features like ways to manufacture a heater from a durable film, and rotary connectors that provide the electrical connection from the rotating steering wheel back to the dash board. That search cost the client a couple hundred dollars, and saved him maybe ten thousand dollars.

A patent search is like an insurance policy. It reduces the risk that you might waste big bucks on a patent application, only to find out that it was unpatentable. It can't eliminate all the risk, because no search is perfect. For a search to catch 99% of all relevant "prior art" (which is what we call any technology that pre-dates your invention), it could cost more than a patent application and take longer to prepare.

Patent searches add to the overall cost of the process. But they do provide advantages other than preventing investing in an unpatentable invention.

For instance, the search results help to educate both the inventor and the patent attorney. My client can learn about some related technology that he might not have known about, which may mean getting information about his competitors' products, or even ideas of how to improve his own. Of course, he needs to be careful about adopting ideas from unexpired patents, so he doesn't infringe the rights of others.

A patent search helps me as the Patent Attorney to focus the strategy of the patent application. My client might wishfully assume that his broad concept of a heated steering wheel is patentable. A search may tell us that the concept is already well known, but lets us focus on a particular aspect of his invention that still may be patentable. I can write a patent application that focuses its attention on that feature, and we may even save a round of rejections (and thus thousands of dollars).

But a patent search is not always needed or recommended. If my client comes to me soon before the filing deadline, there won't be time for a search. Two months is as close as you should cut it when a search may be needed. If you know about the deadline, consider searching well in advance, deferring the patent application decision until a little later.

A search might not be worth the cost and time when the technology is hard to search, or so new that we know there won't be anything in the patent search database, or when my client is sure they know the history and current market for the technology. That's a judgment call my clients and I make together.

Another caution about patent searching is that most searches just look at the database of issued patents and published patent applications. This is a great database, except that not every pertinent "prior art" technology has been patented. The reality is that we search there because it's easy to find things there. Kind of like the drunk who lost his car keys down the street, but searches under the lamp-post a block away because "the light's better here." Maybe it's not that bad, but it's why I suggest supplementing a patent search with an Internet search, and advise my clients to research their own industry references for other possible prior art.

A "full search" usually involves my office hiring a search specialist who works in Washington DC, and who searches the Patent and Trademark Office records directly. Of course, I can do an online search, but not all technology lends itself to word searches. Sure, you can search "heated steering wheel" and find most of the patent titles. But when you have an invention that consists of a flange that protrudes laterally instead of the traditional vertical protrusion, then you need somebody to flip through the patents in that technology area, and look at the images, not just the words in the title and text.

Chapter 36

Patentability Versus Infringement

All this talk about patent searching has referred to a "Patentability search" that answers the question, "Is this invention patentable?" It's important to know that this is an entirely separate question from whether the new product will infringe someone else's patent. A patentability search asks, "Can I stop others from using my invention?" while an infringement search asks, "Do I have the right to produce this product?" These two concepts are independent, because you may be able to patent your invention, but are unable to sell it because some aspect also infringes another patent. Or, you may be unable to patent it, yet still have the right to sell it (or any other combination of circumstances).

Sometimes, a client will call me to talk about patenting a new product. Then, he gets worried that the new product might infringe someone else's patent. He'll often ask me if we should search to make sure the new product doesn't infringe someone else's patent. The answer is almost always, "Don't bother."

The only time an infringement or "right to use" search makes sense is when you have some reason to believe there is a real risk. Like when you have a close competitor who's aggressive about getting patents. Or someone had made veiled threats about patent infringement. Or maybe if you're about to invest massive sums in tooling or marketing that you couldn't afford to walk away from. But infringement searches are much more involved and expensive than patentability searches, and are not routinely done.

Chapter 37

What About Foreign Patents?

Few of my clients pursue foreign protection, because it's rarely economically justified. They're satisfied protecting the U.S. market and enjoying the peripheral benefits discussed earlier, because a U.S. patent can provide some real effect in other markets, even if it doesn't allow you to sue overseas. If you thought patent litigation was expensive, inconvenient, and uncertain in the U.S., imagine spending months of your life in China or France, embroiled in patent litigation!

But for very valuable inventions, where a foreign nation's market is significant, a foreign patent may be worth pursuing. One of my clients has developed a rifle that's a direct competitor of one made by a Belgian company. To prevent that competitor from making his improved design in their usual factory, he chose to pursue a Belgian patent. The competitor can still open a factory in, say, Mexico, and sell to customers in the Middle East, but that would be an inconvenience and expense. My client probably hopes that the Belgian company would rather pay him a reasonable royalty to get permission to make the improved design in their own factory.

Here are the key things you need to know about foreign patent rights, in case you might ever want to pursue them:

1. Remember that one-year grace period to file in the U.S. after your first public activity? Sorry, but foreign nations don't grant you that. If your invention is published before you file an application somewhere, you lose foreign rights (same as if you brought the invention into the foreign nation).

Lesson: Talk to your patent attorney about it while the invention is still secret.

2. A filed ("pending") U.S. patent application preserves the foreign option. You have a year of breathing time after your U.S. filing to decide whether to file overseas. But your U.S. application must be filed before you publicize the invention (including on the Internet) or you lose foreign rights under rule 1 above.

3. There is no "worldwide patent." However, international patent treaties allow you to file an application (called a "PCT" for the Patent Cooperation Treaty) that initially covers many nations, and which buys you time to decide which nations you want to pursue to the end. But even though this consolidates some aspects of the examination, you still eventually need to get a translation for each nation, and have final approval in each patent office. The European Union has a comparable process.

4. Foreign patent protection is very expensive. Patent protection in even a moderate number of foreign nations can easily cost six figures. Even a single nation can be at least as expensive as the initial U.S. patent application, even though all the patent writing brain-work has been done. That's why even the best-funded multinational companies don't pursue foreign patents on most of their inventions.

Chapter 38

The Patent Process in Brief

"No battle plan ever survives contact with the enemy."
—Field Marshall Helmuth Carl Bernard von Moltke.

A good patent application is like a battle plan. It anticipates all the possible rejections, and it's stocked with all the ammunition that may be needed to overcome those possible rejections. But once a patent application is filed, anything can happen.

Here are the rules of thumb (and there are many exceptions to the rules).

1. Most of my clients get their patent, and one that provides some real protection.

2. Almost every application is rejected the first time around.

3. It takes, on average, about 2 years from application filing to patent issuance.

4. Patent and Trademark Office examiners are "variable." Some are talented, some barely speak English. Some give great attention to your application, others don't even appear to have read it. It's sometimes frustrating, but it's reality.

5. The budget for patent "prosecution" (the argument and modification process) is typically less than the application cost, maybe about half.

6. Contrary to press reports of "bad" patents being improperly issued, "good" patents are hard to get. Even the most talented Patent Attorney often has to fight tooth and nail to get an important invention

patented. I wish I had a nickel for every time a client said, "Why can't you get me one of those "bad" patents on an unpatentable invention?"!

Chapter 39

The Long-Winded Version of the Patent Process

When I accept a new client, I send a long letter that explains many of the likely scenarios that can arise in the patent process. Even serious business owners can get a little over-enthusiastic about their invention, so I like to bring a client back to reality, so there's no disappointment later. Some people would call that a "CYA" letter, but I think most business owners appreciate knowing the reality of what might be down the road.

Here's the key excerpt of what I tell my new clients in that long letter (costs are based on 2008 economics):

The first Patent and Trademark Office action will arrive about a year or so after we file the patent application. (I've had cases where this took four years, so there's plenty of uncertainty!) In almost every case, including those that eventually yield successful results, all the claims are rejected.

Depending on the case and the examiner, there'll be rejections or objections to minor informalities that are easily corrected, as well as substantive rejections citing prior art documents such as patents. These rejections usually go claim by claim, and conclude that each claim is either lacking in "novelty" or is "obvious" in view of a combination of the cited references.

Sometimes, where there are two or more independent inventions in a single application, the examiner may issue a "Restriction Requirement." This requires us to choose which of the multiple inventions is to be searched and examined. The other invention may be pursued by filing a "Divisional" application, pursuing those claims. This has the disadvantage of another filing fee, and future issue and maintenance fees, in addition to the added cost of my time to handle a second case and its documentation. For many businesses, however, having a greater quantity of patents in your portfolio adds perceived value (see my client's IPO story earlier) and can even impress competitors who are more worried about being sued under several different patents than they are being sued under one patent.

Sometime within six months to two years after filing the application (normally about a year), we receive an "Office action," which is the communication sent by the Patent and Trademark Office examiner after his examination, which rejects or allows the claims. The attorney time and cost to respond to an Office action varies widely. A simple action requiring only formal changes can be less than $1000. An action with many rejections, citing many different references, and requiring changes to the claim strategy, plus legal or technical arguments can exceed $5000.

Sometimes, there will be several alternative strategic paths available, each with a different prospect for success, a different scope of protection to be obtained, and a different cost. One classic dilemma is whether to "take what they're giving us" or to keep fighting. The decision often depends on whether the technology has unusual competitive value to the applicant. The typical case will involve a substantive first response (which may include new claims, amended claims, changed strategy and legal and technical arguments) in the $2000–6000 range, and a second minor response to address remaining issues in the $1000–2000 range.

Sometimes, an examiner will be just plain wrong, and my client and I will both agree on it. These are the cases in the worst 25% in terms of cost and time delays. In these cases, we'll make our best case, and face a second Office action that will normally be made "Final." This means that the examiner is no longer obliged to consider any more of our arguments. In practical terms, it means that we must pay another filing fee (with a "Continuation" application) to "take another bite at the apple."

It's widely believed that the Patent and Trademark Office's policies for compensating examiners give them an incentive to reject a legitimately patentable case to generate a second filing fee. Sometimes, these are allowed after the second fee is paid. Other times, a substantive response by us will be required to address new rejections (because sometimes when we beat the initial rejections, they replace them with new ones), with costs as above for substantive first responses. Another frustrating possibility is that we successfully argue around a rejection, then the examiner comes up with a new rejection he should have raised the first time, putting us back at square one.

In a minority of the worst quarter of cases, perhaps less than 10% of the time, we will face rejections that cannot be overcome through the normal process, either due to an unjustifiably stubborn examiner, or due to our choosing to fight an uphill battle against tough but borderline rejections, or due to a genuinely proper rejection. If all of our best arguments have been made on the record, and the formal rejections have been addressed, we then face the choice of appealing or abandoning our efforts. An appeal is a very extensive (and expensive) process that can exceed the typical cost of the patent application, and may sit unheard for several years in the Patent and Trademark Office. Appeal costs vary widely depending on the scope of issues that remain in dispute. If an appeal within the Patent and Trademark Office fails, there are more avenues for appeal in the courts.

Fortunately, the Patent and Trademark Office recently adopted a new process by which we can file a "warning shot" appeal that costs a lot less than an full appeal, and gives the examiner (and his or her supervisors) a chance to look at the case much more seriously before the extensive legal briefs are prepared. That has been a real improvement for many of my clients.

In the easiest quarter of cases, the first action will still include a rejection of most or all claims, but which may be overcome relatively easily with some minor clarifications, or quick adjustments in strategy. The cost for these is at or below the lower end of the normal cost range, to get to allowance. Once in a blue moon (~1% of the time) we will see a "first action allowance." In these happy cases, our first concern often is that we did not try aggressively enough to gain broad coverage.

After all the claims are allowed, the issue fee of about $1000 is due, and maintenance fees are payable at 3.5 years ($465), 7.5 years ($1180), and 11.5 years ($1955), plus my nominal charges to monitor, notify, and administer payment. All these fees will likely to have increased by the time they come due, and assume a small company with less than 500 employees. Big companies pay double, thanks to Congress, which also actually takes for its own spending some of the fees paid by patent applicants—a true tax on innovation!

With all these costs and uncertainties, it's important that my clients take a realistic look at how much profit a patent is likely to bring, and discount that by the risk that the patent might never be granted. Even though my track record is much better than 50%, I suggest that clients at least double the total patent budget to account for all the uncertainties. If the patent isn't going to add at least $25,000–40,000 in added profit over the next few years (or increase the company buy-out value by that much) then the investment probably isn't economically justified.

Chapter 40

Why Create a Family of Patent Applications?

Here's an advanced topic I'm putting in this book to help me advise my clients. Often, I need to explain the options for creating a family of patent applications, and now I can just point you to this page.

A simple patent application is filed, is prosecuted, and issues. That's it. But in many cases the story is more complex.

Divisional Applications

When the examiner looks at an application and thinks he'll need to search and examine more than one invention, he'll issue a "Restriction Requirement" that basically says "pick one invention." The patent filing fee pays for only one invention to be searched. So if we have an application claiming both an apparatus and a method of manufacturing, maybe we'll decide to pursue the claims to the apparatus itself right now, and leave the claims to the method of manufacturing for later.

We then have the option to file a Divisional application with the claims we elected not to pursue. Usually, we wait on this and see how the prosecution of the first case goes. It usually gives us insight into how to argue the second case, and defer the expense. But like all the related applications, it will expire 20 years after the first "parent" application in the family was filed.

"Continuation" Applications

Often, I succeed in getting my client only some of the patent protection we really think is deserved. The examiner agrees to allow some of the claims, but not the broadest ones that would provide the best value. Here are the options when this happens:

1. We can take what they're giving us, and live with it.

2. We can pay another filing fee and argue some more for the rejected claims, while carrying along the allowed claims (we file a "Request for Continued Examination" or "RCE".) This makes sense when the client is in no rush to have the patent issue, and wants to limit future maintenance fees, which would be doubled if he had two issued patents instead of one.

3. Do both. We can file a spin-off application (a "Continuation") in which we will fight for the rejected claims (maybe even appeal) and let the first application issue with the halfway decent claims. This is good if my client needs some protection now, like when there's an infringer out there that needs to be stopped. If the second application is granted, it means having two patents in the portfolio instead of one, which may impress investors, but doubles the maintenance fees that will be due over time.

A Powerful Strategy for "Crown Jewel" Inventions

For a crown-jewel invention of great value, one which may be likely to face infringers, I advise a special Continuation strategy. Imagine my everyday challenge—trying to write patent claims to be sure they cover the invention so that a competitor's future product is covered by them. I want claims to be broad, but not so broad that they get rejected or invalidated. Yet I can't know just what the competitor's future product would look like. Often, I've looked at other patents my client was worried about infringing, and found that there was no infringement because of the terminology the patent lawyer used. If they'd used different wording, my client would have been shut down, but after a patent is granted, the language can't be changed.

Imagine if I could draft a new set of patent claims *after* seeing the competitor's new product! It would be a breeze to make sure the product was covered by the new claims (as long as it really did use the key inventive concept). That would be a wonderful gift of hindsight.

If we play our cards right, we can do exactly that. Let's say we get solid patent protection on an important invention, and we are pretty darn satisfied with the protection. Still, we can file a Continuation application before the patent issues and half-heartedly argue for broader or different protection. We take our time in all the communications, so for limited expense can buy a couple years of time when a "member of the patent family" is pending.

As long as that "child" application (or one of its children—we can repeat the process over and over) is pending, we preserve the right to draft claims targeted to an infringing device. And those claims will be like a lethal rifle shot aimed at the competitor's product, not the broad shotgun blast we normally use for patent claims.

Of course, this can cost several thousands of dollars a year to keep this option alive, but when you're anticipating a half-million dollar litigation bill, you'll be glad you gave yourself this strategically sophisticated option. The reason I try to persuade my clients to use this approach isn't to generate legal fees; it's because if they have to litigate, I want them to *win*. (Or at least have infringers be effectively scared off by the power of this strategy.)

When You Improve the Invention After the Application Is Filed.

Typically, inventions keep evolving, and products keep improving. Creative people don't stop thinking the moment an application is filed. And even an incremental improvement can be patentable.

But the disclosure part of a patent application can't be changed after it's filed. (We can change the claims language and strategy, but only to reflect concepts that were in the original application.) That means that if we want protection for something new, we need to file another patent application.

There's a handy tool for this situation, and it's called a "Continuation-In-Part" (CIP) application. It lets us clone the old application, add in some new material, and file it, while the original ("parent") application is still pending.

If we choose, we can leave in the application the parent's claims (which go back to the original filing date) and add in the claims to the new features, dropping the parent application and just prosecuting the "updated" application. Or, we can let the two applications run in parallel. Because you can modify claims in a patent application, lots of different scenarios can apply, and your Patent Attorney can suggest strategies that meet your needs in each case.

One suggestion with CIP applications: To economize, we don't rush filing the moment an improvement arises. You may wish to wait a little while if development is continuing, and accumulate a bunch improvements in a single CIP filing, which reduces filing fees and legal fees. Of course, an incremental improvement is an invention like any other, and all the important deadlines apply. You need to file a CIP within one year of the time the improved version is made public or offered for sale.

Chapter 41

Patent Conflicts in the Real World

When an infringement accusation arises, it generally follows a typical pattern.

First, the accusation is made. The patent owner may informally tell the accused (who will rush to his lawyer to get advice), or the patent owner may have his lawyer send a formal accusation letter that includes a copy of the patent in question. The formal accusation establishes certain rights to collect damages after that point.

The defending patent attorney will analyze the patent and give his client an opinion on whether the patent owner has a case. There may be negotiations back and forth between the lawyers, which may end up in a settlement.

If the case for infringement is strong, the accused will normally agree to stop infringing. Often, the patent owner will grant a time for the infringer to sell off inventory, encouraging the accused to settle instead of litigating. For cases like this, it's almost unheard of for the infringer to pay damages or attorney fees. Sometimes, the patent owner will allow the accused to continue production, but by paying a royalty under a license agreement that's negotiated.

If the case for infringement is weak, the defending attorney may simply convince the patent owner's lawyer that the case is too weak and maybe that the patent would be invalidated if litigated.

Reexamination

If the accused has any documents that would invalidate the patent (prior art that should have been considered by the examiner but wasn't) they have another good option.

They can file (or threaten) a "reexamination" of the patent, which essentially reopens the case, and gives the patent examiner another chance to reject the patent based on new evidence. This requires a stiff Patent and Trademark Office fee of thousands of dollars, but is far cheaper than litigating the validity of the patent in court. In some cases, the patent owner might agree to accept a painlessly small royalty from the accused infringer to make the threat of invalidation go away.

Royalties

When royalties are to be paid to gain permission under a patent license, the deal may be structured in just about any way you can imagine: Percentage of profits, percent of revenue, dollars per sale. There may be caps, minimums, flat annual fees, or any combination thereof. There's no "typical" royalty rate. That's negotiated, and the parties consider how important the invention is to the product and how much profit it adds. The licensee (the manufacturer) has to do all the work and take all the risk, so the patent owner shouldn't expect to get more than a minor fraction of the profit.

Sometimes, when a patent owner decides not to get "greedy" and sets the royalty rate at a level that I would describe as "painless," he can attract lots of licensees, maybe even making his invention ubiquitous. To state the obvious: A billion pennies is worth more than a million dollars.

Litigation

In a small minority of cases, litigation is needed, because the parties just can't agree, and both sides can afford to fight. In these situations there's usually a lot of business value at stake. Personally, I choose not make litigation part of my practice, because I prefer an independent practice that focuses on technology and creating important legal rights for my clients. I advise on patent infringement, conduct settlement negotiations, and prepare licensing agreements, but I keep out of the courtroom. Patent litigation requires fielding an army, and I prefer to stay independent. Besides, I think the experience of litigation simply sucks, whether as a plaintiff, defendant, or lawyer.

I tell my clients, "it's often better to lose a negotiation than to win a litigation." But in case any lawyers for my client's adversaries are reading this, they should know that I'm simply explaining what any savvy business owner knows, which is that litigation always costs more than you think, wins are rarely as satisfying or profitable as hoped, and good cases can still be lost. Not to mention that for a business owner, the months (or years) spent in litigation represent heartburn, lost sleep, stress, and distraction from the business of your business.

Damages

If a patent is litigated, and it's ruled to be infringed, damages may be awarded. Courts have lots of way of calculating damages, probably as many different ways as we can calculate a royalty. But the award is usually painful to the defendant and disappointing to the plaintiff. If you face litigation from either side, your attorney can also advise about the chances for recovering your attorney fees if you win or paying if you lose.

The Triple Threat That Makes Patents More Powerful

There's one aspect of patent law that makes infringers more likely to respect your patent rights, even if they know you hate the idea of suing. It's called "treble damages." Treble damages are awarded when an infringer willfully continues infringing after accused, without any legal justification. If that occurs, you don't just get the profits they earned from infringing, you get triple the profits! That is a profound threat that makes infringers a lot less likely to cross their fingers and hope you don't sue.

The only way to avoid liability for treble damages is if you have a legitimate argument that you were not infringing (even if you lost the litigation). And that requires that you get a formal "non-infringement opinion" from a competent patent attorney at the outset when accused. If you have no case, then no attorney will stake his reputation on it for your benefit. But if it's a close case with arguments to be made on both sides, then the accused will probably be able to get this kind of "insurance policy" that will protect them against paying treble damages, even if he loses the lawsuit.

Of course, when clients ask me about whether they infringe a patent (and are not facing imminent litigation), I typically give an informal real-world opinion that gives them the information they need, without the expensive level of detail that provides the insurance against treble damages.

Chapter 42

Employees and Patent Ownership

It's important that businesses with employees use employment agreements that provide that the employer gets the rights to any inventions the employee may create. This should include inventions made outside of work hours and may even include technologies that are unrelated to the business core technology. (You can always be reasonable later and allow an employee to pursue a patent on his own for an invention relating to his hobby or other unrelated technology that doesn't compete with you.)

The agreement should have the employee agree to cooperate and sign all needed documents needed for the company to gain patent rights, even after the employment with your company ceases. Your general business or employment lawyer should be able to provide suitable documents, but if they are uncertain about patent rights questions, then you may wish to have your patent attorney advise.

Patent Assignments and Ownership

Normally, my clients with inventor/employees will have me prepare an Assignment that transfers ownership of the invention to the company (or its designated holding entity). This is normally signed at the same time the application is signed for filing. Even self-employed inventors may assign the invention to their own company.

However, many companies are missing a powerful opportunity to employ a more advanced corporate structuring strategy. The right strategy can protect a business and its ongoing operations against lawsuits that could otherwise cripple it.

Imagine your business loses a lawsuit because a customer was injured using or misusing your product, or maybe an employee caused a traffic fatality on the job. Now imagine that to pay the judgment, you need to sell your patent assets. That's as good as going bankrupt, because then you'll no longer have the right to make your own products. How to avoid this risk?

The Asset Protection section of this book will explain how holding your patents and other intellectual property in a separate company can insulate them against loss in lawsuits. Even if your operating/manufacturing company were bankrupted, your patent holding company would still exist, so you could start a new operating company from scratch (even using the same trademarks!). It's powerful, simple, and a strategy worth learning about.

Chapter 43

How to Select a Patent Attorney

Hiring a patent attorney is like hiring a ghost writer for your autobiography. He's going to tell the story of your invention, so you'd better be sure he's qualified to understand it and to make the story compelling to a patent examiner. There are over 30,000 registered patent attorneys and patent agents. (Agents lack a law degree, but have the other qualifications.) How to pick one?

A word-of mouth referral from an active client of a particular patent attorney is an excellent way to find a good patent attorney.

You can try picking a local patent attorney from the Yellow pages and rely on your in-person instincts on whether they'll do the quality work you need. But I advise not to limit yourself geographically, and instead to try to hire the best attorney, no matter where he is located. I choose to live in the mountains where there happens to be no tech clients nearby, so clearly I'm biased on this issue!

Working long distance is rarely a concern. The only time I see most of my firearms clients face-to-face is at the SHOT Show.

It's good to find a specialist who understands your technology and who can be more creative and aggressive about the possible scope of protection. Sometimes, you might have a feeling that your product is new and valuable, but you need your patent attorney to help figure out exactly what the patentable aspect might be. It's nice when he already knows the technology.

A specialist well-suited to your technology is desirable, but the patent attorney needs to avoid direct conflicts of interest, so if you're a direct competitor of one of his existing clients, he'll be unable to represent you. He'll also initially want to know a little about your invention in order to confirm that there is no conflict, before he hears too many of your secrets. But otherwise, you can trust any patent attorney to keep all your secrets, because we'd lose our licenses if we ever violated our duty of confidentiality.

You can find patent attorneys at large law firms or with small or solo practices. The downside of the large firm is that you can't be sure which attorney will be assigned to your project, and if you're a new, small client, your high-priced patent may be used as a training exercise for an inexperienced new hire. The downside of a solo is the concern that he's a solo because he couldn't get a decent job. You hope that he's top-notch, but just prefers to be independent of the law firm rat race. Look at his other clients, because a struggling solo will lack ongoing relationships with prominent clients.

Some of my clients hesitated before they hired me because I didn't have a big firm of litigators down the hallway. I explain that if it's ever necessary to put together a litigation team, I'll help out with that process and be just as much (or little) a part of the litigation effort as needed. In reality, the guy who writes your patents in the big firms probably isn't going to litigate your case either.

Hiring an independent makes sense if you are planning to build a long-term relationship. At big firms, lawyers quit and go to other firms, or quit to go in-house with clients (this happened all the time during the dot-com boom). An independent is much more likely to be content with his practice away from the rat-race, and unless he's ready to retire, is going to be the one answering your calls for a long time to come.

Hiring a prominent independent patent attorney (such as yours truly) can be an ideal choice, if not the cheapest choice. However, such attorneys will generally limit their practices only to established companies or other "serious" clients. Individual inventors and small privately-held companies will normally be asked for a retainer before the process gets much beyond a brief phone conference. Email inquiries are also welcome, although the author is unable to give legal advice without having formalized an attorney-client relationship.

Cost can be a major factor, and a patent attorney should give you a rough idea of the cost, and a firm quote on a specific project phase. The reality is that good attorneys charge top fees because they're busy. A deep discount may mean that an attorney is struggling for clients for reasons that might make you wonder about their abilities. But if you get a cost estimate that is much higher than expected, be sure to ask why, to be sure that the attorney hasn't misunderstood the scope of your invention or your objectives.

Many small inventors ask me if I can help find a company to buy or license their patent. I try to help if I have any ideas, but there's little a patent attorney can do. The reality is that few inventors find success with so-called "invention marketing companies" and are much better off marketing their inventions themselves. Also, it's extremely rare for an attorney to accept a share of a client's invention in lieu of their normal fees. I made an exception for my brother, once, but that's about it!

Your First Patent Attorney Meeting

You found an attorney that seems right for your technology, and you've told him a little bit about your invention in a telephone call (which he probably didn't charge you for). Now you're going to hire him and start the patent process.

The attorney will need to see any documentation you have so he can better understand the scope of the invention. That will let him quote the cost to prepare and file the patent application. Your documentation may include written descriptions, drawings, and anything else that can help make the technology clear. The clearer and more detailed your documentation, the less time-consuming the project will appear to the attorney, and the lower the quote will likely be.

Don't worry about writing a long-winded document. What counts is simply a clear, complete disclosure of all the important features and advantages in your invention, how it works, how it's manufactured, and what makes it different from existing technology. For mechanical inventions like firearms, drawings (whether sketches on cocktail napkins or CAD drawings) are most critical. The patent attorney will need different views to explain all the features of the invention. A moving mechanism such as a firearm action might be shown as a sequence of images showing the different steps of the operation.

Drafting and Reviewing the Patent Application

Your patent attorney will then tell you if anything else is needed, including other drawing views. Then, the patent application process can proceed, with the attorney creating a first draft for the inventor to review for completeness and accuracy. The drafting process can take a month or two because a patent application is an extensive document written from scratch, and is not merely a form to fill out as a few novices sometimes assume. However, if there's a critical filing deadline, your patent attorney should be able to do whatever it takes to protect your invention.

The drafted application may have some blanks to fill in and questions to answer, and will typically be accompanied by rough or informal drawings. I offer the following advice to the inventor who's about to review my work:

You should resist the instinct to trust a formal-looking (and hopefully well-written) document in an unfamiliar format as "correct." As the patent attorney, my job is simply to write the story of your invention, and that's a story you know best. Therefore, you should scrutinize all the facts and assumptions I made, which will undoubtedly have some errors. You should be sure that you understand and agree with everything in the application, and that it's entirely complete.

It's very important that you be attuned to any possible detail that may have been left out. Reading the application draft may even give you ideas you have not had before, and these can be included now. Of particular importance are the drawings and the "Detailed Description" portions. These are important because once the application is filed, no new matter may be added. If we make an error or omission in these areas, it won't be correctable later. Keep in mind that extra details and specific examples in this section won't narrow the scope of protection, but can provide a more robust foundation for patent protection.

The Claims at the end define the hoped-for scope of protection. They're written in an archaic but precise format. Some inventors choose to delve into them and advise the attorney if they think that any of the independent claims (the ones that do not refer back to another claim number) include an element or detail that's not essential to the invention. We don't want to make it easy for competitors to design around a claim with a product that omits one unnecessarily-claimed feature. Other inventors don't worry about the claims, which can be changed later as needed to avoid rejection, as long as the changes are supported by details in the original description and drawings.

After I get back the inventor's comments, I prepare a final version with documents for signature, and when I get those back, I file the application as soon as possible.

Then, we wait a year or more for the first real word from the Patent and Trademark Office on the nature of the first round of rejections.

The vast majority of applications I file eventually overcome the rejections and issue as patents, typically about 2 years after filing. Then, my client can put the patent number on the patented product to notify competitors that the product is not a safe candidate for a knock-off.

Chapter 44

Conclusion:
Key Patent Points

1. If it's new and valuable, get an expert opinion before ruling out patentability. You may be surprised what's patentable.

2. Keep good records of your inventing. Whoever has the best evidence that they were the first to invent an idea wins the patent battle.

3. When you reveal your invention, pay close attention to the one-year deadline to file the patent application.

4. Finally, learn the Inventor's Prayer:

"Dear Lord, please help me to keep my damned mouth shut for one more day!"

Section III:
BUSINESS
STRUCTURE
AND
ASSET
PROTECTION

Chapter 45

The Five Things I Wish Every Business Owner Knew About Protecting Their Assets

1. Incorporate. This is obvious, and most businesses do it. But startup owners can get a painful lesson if they delay this critical way to protect their personal assets from business liabilities.

2. Divide and Conquer. If you have equipment and intellectual property, get it safely out of your operating business to protect it from lawsuits.

3. LLCs are Essential. Consider using an LLC instead of a corporation. You get better protection from personal lawsuits and fewer corporate formalities to deal with.

4. Plan Ahead. You must do asset protection planning well before you need it. It's too late to plan after you've been sued.

5. Prepare a Buy-Sell agreement. If your business partner dies, the lack of a Buy-Sell agreement may leave you doing business with your business partner's heirs.

Chapter 46

How Failing to Incorporate Can Lead to Needless Financial Ruin

Sam Silliman began manufacturing firearms in a building out in back of his garage. He got all the necessary licenses from the government and builds custom-made rifles for people with money to burn.

Sam didn't bother to form a corporation or an LLC to run his business; he hates lawyers and didn't want to spend money on forming a separate business entity. Sam spends his afternoons in his shop with his old Bridgeport and Hardinge, doing the precision work he loves. His rifles are very popular, and word of mouth from satisfied clients keeps demand for his product high.

Last year, one of Sam's rifles malfunctioned after misuse, resulting in the gun owner being facially disfigured.

And if the bad publicity the incident brought weren't enough, Sam got a knock at the door on a recent Saturday morning.

"Process server. You've been served," said the fat man standing at the door.

As the man's dilapidated car turned around in Sam's driveway and left in a cloud of blue smoke, Sam glanced at the demand letter: One million dollars! His heart sank, and dozens of thoughts ran through his head at once.

Sam didn't have a million dollars—not even close! But he did have his house, and a wife and kids to support. How was he ever going to afford a lawyer to defend this suit? Even though business was good, there still wasn't a lot left over at the end of the month.

Monday morning, Sam called his insurance agent. The conversation did little to improve his mood. Sam's homeowner's insurance policy didn't cover anything Sam did in his business life—it was strictly for personal liabilities, such as the dog biting a visitor, that sort of thing.

Trying not to show his panic to his family, Sam made an appointment to see a lawyer. Reviewing the demand, the lawyer asked if Sam had formed a separate entity for his business. "Well no, I didn't want to spend the money. And besides, it wouldn't have prevented this lawsuit, anyway."

The lawyer replied that perhaps it would not have prevented the lawsuit, but noted that if Sam hadn't done business in his own name, he wouldn't be faced with the prospect of losing his home.

"Forming a separate business entity is like building a wall between your business and personal assets, Sam," said the lawyer. "If you'd formed a separate entity, then the only thing you'd be looking at losing are the assets in your business—and what's that, a few machine tools? In hindsight, it would have been a smart thing to do . . ."

"Well, can't I form one now?" asked Sam.

"Well . . . sure . . . but you still have liability for all the things your business did in the years before you formed the business entity," said his lawyer. "So if there's another accident with one of your guns that was purchased before you started using your business entity, you're still liable, I'm afraid."

Sam wisely took his lawyer's advice and immediately formed a business entity: Silliman Rifles, LLC. Sam began running his business with the new entity.

Still, after two years of litigation and over $100,000 in attorney's fees, Sam was found liable for making a product that was dangerously defective, and the plaintiff was awarded one million dollars to compensate him for his damages.

In order to pay the judgment, Sam had to sell his house, liquidate his personal assets, and declare bankruptcy. Now the family lives with his wife's parents—with whom Sam does not particularly get along—as they try to scrape up enough money for a down payment on a new house.

Silliman still makes beautiful rifles, but Sam has learned a very painful lesson in the process.

How Sam Could Have Avoided Disaster

Let's look at how things might have turned out differently if Sam had formed Silliman Rifles, LLC when he started his business.

Sam would have visited a corporate attorney, and spent about $2500 setting up his corporation, including paying the lawyer, the state filing fees, and so forth.

Because his business is high-risk, he follows his lawyer's advice and forms a separate entity, Silliman Holdings LLC, to own his machine tools, to keep those assets out of the operating business (more on that later). Silliman Rifles, LLC leases the equipment from Silliman Holdings, LLC, so the business has no assets to lose in the event it is sued as a result of a client getting injured with one of Sam's rifles.

Sam opens a bank account in the name of the business, and does not mix his business and personal funds. He pays himself a salary every month, and scrupulously keeps his business assets and personal assets completely separate.

Now, having bulletproofed his business the best he can, Sam gets sued and still spends two years and $100,000 defending the lawsuit. He loses and is ordered to pay $1 million.

But Sam's business and personal assets are separate, and the operating business doesn't have any assets in its own name, so Sam offers only $100,000, telling the plaintiff's attorney, "Well, you can take this, or I'll just declare bankruptcy for Silliman Rifles, LLC. Your choice."

The plaintiff wisely agrees to accept this low-ball offer, Sam pays the judgment out of one year's profits, and goes on with business as usual. He keeps his house (and doesn't have to live with his in-laws!), and his business continues intact, profitable as ever.

How to Ruin the Day
of a Bottom-Feeding Trial Lawyer:
The Lawsuit That Never Happened

Here's how Sam's bulletproofed business might have led to an even sweeter result for Sam.

The plaintiff's greedy trial lawyer, who takes cases on contingency (and therefore only goes after defendants with money), does a routine asset search on Sam and on Silliman Firearms, LLC. He learns that Silliman Firearms LLC is formed in a particular state with very good creditor protection (more on that later). He also finds out that Silliman Firearms LLC has no assets other than a business checking account with a nominal amount in it.

Since contingency lawyers get paid only if there are assets to grab, there's nothing in it for this lawyer.

"Sorry," the lawyer tells the potential plaintiff, "but I can't take this case on a contingency basis. If you'd like to give me a retainer of $20,000, we can get started. But I'm not sure that we're going to be able to collect from this business; it doesn't have any assets to liquidate to pay you."

The plaintiff doesn't want to pony up the cash and gives up on the lawsuit. Why sue if you can't get any money?

The lawsuit never happened. The process server never drove up Sam's driveway. Sam never had a "bad day." Sam didn't spend a penny defending a lawsuit.

This is why smart businesses set up proper business entities at the beginning.

They keep business assets separate from personal assets, which helps protect your personal assets from any business liabilities that might arise. It can mean the difference between losing your house and brokerage account, and keeping them safe and sound.

Chapter 47

The Amazingly Simple Business Structure That Provides Essential Lawsuit Protection

Even if you do form a separate business entity to run your business, if you hold all your business assets in the same entity as the operating business, you can lose all your business assets when your business gets sued. Here's an example:

Jack Hush owns Silent Knight, Inc., a successful company that specializes in the manufacture of firearms suppressors. Jack took the reins of the company from his father, who retired after more than 30 years in the business.

Jack's father prudently took what he thought were great pains to have everything set up properly. He did everything his old business lawyer told him. He incorporated the business in Oregon, where the company is located, and kept careful financial records. He never took money from the business to pay the home mortgage and never used company funds to pay for non-business items. Over the years, Silent Knight has grown and prospered due to smart business practices and a very loyal workforce, all of whom have been with the company for more than 10 years.

Silent Knight, Inc. owns a fair amount of intellectual property (IP) because it has worked diligently over the years with a skilled patent and trademark attorney. Silent Knight carefully polices its brands, and sends stern letters those competitors who stray into their brand's territory. They have a program to reward employees who submit invention disclosures that lead to patents. They know how important their IP is in the sometimes-cutthroat firearms industry.

However, Jack's old business lawyer never told Jack that it's not a good idea to own the IP in the operating business, an omission for which Jack will later pay dearly.

One Monday, Jack gets a letter in the mail from a law firm. He is being sued for "causing an injury" to someone who actually misused one of his products. Jack immediately faxes the letter to his business attorney and asks him to get the details of the case as soon as possible.

About a week later, his attorney calls him. "Jack, apparently the guy and his buddy were injured when he tried to use a Silent Knight .22 pistol can on a high-powered varmint rifle. Can you believe that? Maybe he thought he'd be able to shoot the prairie dogs without ears and hear the bullet strikes. Moron."

Jack couldn't believe that anyone would be so stupid. After all, the safety literature enclosed with each Silent Knight suppressor warns of the danger of trying to use a suppressor for any weapon that is not of the caliber specified on the suppressor.

"So," Jack asked, "what happened to the guy?" Jack listened while his attorney told about the extent of the guy's injuries—it was pretty horrific, really. Jack felt sick to his stomach.

"He's claiming $5 million in injuries and damages, Jack," said the attorney. "I'm afraid this could tie you up for a long time."

"But he misused the product!" said Jack.

"That doesn't matter, I'm afraid. All he needs is a lefty jury who wants to punish you for making those evil silencers, and you'll be really screwed, Jack."

Two years later, Jack finally loses the case. In addition to the huge sum—over $300,000—that he had to pay his attorneys to defend the case, Jack was found liable for actual damages of $4.3 million dollars, plus punitive damages of another $5 million. For days, he didn't feel like eating, and he couldn't sleep at night.

The injured guy's attorneys came after Silent Knight, Inc. for the judgment amount. Silent Knight, Inc. had assets, so it couldn't just state that its assets exceeded its liabilities and declare bankruptcy. Jack had to sell his company assets—including his equipment and intellectual property—to come up with the money.

As the final indignity, Jack ended up selling his company at auction, to a real blowhard who's loathed throughout the industry. Jack is furious at the idea that this guy now has the right to use the Silent Knight trademark and the patented inventions that Jack worked so hard to create.

How Jack Could Have Kept the Business Operating Profitably, Even After Losing a Big Lawsuit

It's too late for Jack, but the good news for any high-risk business owner is that situations like this can be avoided through a little advance planning. Sure, you can't always prevent getting sued when someone misuses your products, but you can leave as few assets as possible in the "operating company" for their slimy trial attorneys to seize.

To be clear, the "operating company" is the manufacturing or service business that your customers do business with. It's the one they write the checks to.

Here's the secret: What if your operating company owned nothing?

What if all the equipment, real estate, and intellectual property used by the operating business were leased from someone else?

You don't own your building and machine tools; you rent them. You don't own patents and trademarks; you license permission to use them and pay royalties or license fees.

Who owns all those essential business assets? You do. Or rather, a different "holding company" that you own and control owns the assets.

For example, had Jack asked me, I would have advised him that it's insane to have his operating business own anything needed to produce the business income. Especially when you're operating a high-risk business like his.

When the trial lawyers come knocking at your company's door, you don't want to have anything to give them. Jack needs to strip the assets out of the company and put them into another company that he owns.

But Can't They Sue the Holding Company That Sits On All Those Assets?

No, they can't, because they never did business with the holding company, and the holding company never did anything "wrong." After all, when someone driving a rental car hits you, you don't expect to sue Hertz.

Think about how important your intellectual property assets are. Your patents and trademarks represent a valuable asset to the company.

If these were lost through a lawsuit, Jack can't use the Silent Knight brand on any of his products, and can't produce any products using the same ideas and processes that he himself patented—these now belong to the new patent owner.

Without the patents, he couldn't even compete with the new owner of his old assets. And without the trademarks, he's competing against someone who is benefiting from all the good will and reputation Jack built up over the years!

Imagine for a minute what that means to a manufacturer. Anything that you worked to create and patent now is no longer yours to create or use in your business. So you really need to get these out of the operating company where they are vulnerable, and put them into another entity, where they are safe.

So let's say that before he ever gets sued, Jack takes my advice and sets up Silent Knight Holdings, LLC and transfers ownership of the intellectual property to it. He owns all the membership shares and thus has complete control over the IP that the Holdings LLC owns.

Jack decides on a license fee that Silent Knight Inc. will pay to Silent Knight Holdings. I draft up the licensing agreement, and the Silent Knight Inc. bookkeeper writes a check for the licensing fee quarterly.

Jack decides that he's not going to bother doing anything halfway, so he does the same thing for the Silent Knight building and land and the Silent Knight equipment. I advise Jack not to put the real estate into the same LLC that he uses for anything else, since real estate can create its own liabilities. You don't want a repairman who gets injured working on your building to end up owning your patents and trademarks! The equipment might also create its own types of liabilities, so he puts that into a separate LLC as well.

So now what does Silent Knight, Inc. (the original operating company) own? Well, it might still own its accounts receivable. But if those are consistently high, we can create a separate holding company to own those, too.

But let's say that we just leave them in there for the sake of simplicity. Through a bit of planning, we've turned Silent Knight, Inc. into a company not worth suing. This is because if the plaintiff sues and wins, they don't get anything—there's nothing to get! The company has no assets.

Remember how I told you that trial lawyers work on contingency? Do you think a trial lawyer is going to go after a small, privately-held company with no assets? If there's no pot of gold at the end of the rainbow, the trial lawyer is going to ask his client for a fat retainer before he'll begin suing you.

Most of the opportunists looking to sue you can't come up with the money necessary to do that, and what would they gain from that anyway if your company doesn't have any assets to seize?

So, Jack never even gets served with a lawsuit. He's unaware of the accident. He goes merrily on his way, running a profitable business that makes him a very comfortable living year after year and provides high-wage jobs for his loyal employees.

The Painless Lawsuit

What if, despite the fact that the company has no assets, the injured party decides to sue Silent Knight, Inc.?

Well, once the judgment is entered, Silent Knight, Inc. officially becomes bankrupt, which is defined as being unable to meet its debt obligations—one of which is the personal injury judgment. So now, Silent Knight, Inc. can file a Chapter 7 bankruptcy petition, and the bankruptcy trustee will liquidate the few assets of the company to pay off its debts. And all Silent Knight's debts will be wiped out thereafter. Bye-bye, personal injury creditor.

This is all relatively painless because Silent Knight Inc. no longer has any assets except for its accounts receivable. So the bankruptcy trustee collects those, and hands those over to the "secured creditors." These are special creditors who are first in line to receive any proceeds from a bankruptcy. Only then does the personal injury debt get paid.

And then: "Surprise, surprise!" There's nothing left with which to pay the personal injury creditor. It's all gone to the secured creditors. (And an ethical business can make sure all the real obligations and bills are paid, even when the bankruptcy process might not require it.)

What about the IP, the real estate, and the equipment? It's all owned by the holding company, which isn't liable for the debts of the operating company.

The lease agreements that each of these companies signed with Silent Knight, Inc. states very clearly that the lease is to be immediately terminated if Silent Knight, Inc. declares bankruptcy. So now each of those companies is free to pursue a lease of their property with any other company they choose.

Jack, being the manager of all those LLCs he set up to hold the property, decides to lease to another company. Guess which one? The new operating company he has just set up to do business, of course.

Hitting the "Reset Button" After a Lawsuit

Having declared bankruptcy for Silent Knight, Inc., Jack Hush starts up a new company, Hush, LLC. He licenses the IP and the equipment and the real estate to Hush, LLC from his other property-holding LLCs, and he's back in business within the week. But since the holding company still owns all the trademarks, the new company will still be selling "Silent Knight®" suppressors.

Jack didn't even move out of his building. He just had his lawyer draft new employment contracts for his employees in the name of the new company, and he's back in business. Sure, he had to defend a lawsuit, and that was expensive. But it was certainly a better outcome than losing all the business assets, wasn't it?

Many high-risk business owners have very expensive and valuable business property like machinery, equipment, real estate, and intellectual property. Every time you make a sale, your operating business creates liabilities that put this property at risk of seizure by predators if these assets are held in the same entity. This is because if your operating entity is sued, then all the assets of that entity are available to satisfy the judgment.

A side note: These powerful corporate structuring strategies can also protect you from legitimate lawsuits and financial obligations. However, there's nothing to prevent an ethical business from voluntarily meeting all of its obligations.

Rebuilding After Getting Burned

After Sam Silliman's unfortunate legal experience, he knew that that he needed to form an entity to do business, so he formed Silliman Rifles, LLC. This is great for protecting his personal assets, but Sam decides that just isn't good enough.

After having lost just about everything he owned, Sam wasn't about to put his property at risk again. He doesn't have a lot of business property compared to many manufacturers, but what he does have, he'd like to keep if Silliman Rifles gets sued again.

Sam currently owns as his personal property the Silliman trademark and logo, and the machine tools and other equipment that he uses in the business. He knows that if he transfers these from his personal name to Silliman Rifles, LLC, and that LLC is sued, then he could lose the assets. But he also doesn't want to own the property in his own name, because then if he gets sued personally, he could lose his business equipment.

What's Sam to do? Form a separate holding LLC, following the simple yet powerful Bulletproof strategy discussed above.

Sam has his lawyer form a new entity, Silliman Holdings, LLC. He uses this to own the trademark, logo, and the machine tools and equipment. By doing this, Sam has insulated these assets both from the claims of the operating businesses and from any claims against Sam personally.

How does this work, logistically speaking? Well, to keep things on the up and up, Silliman Rifles, LLC ("Rifles") has a lease agreement with Silliman Holdings, LLC ("Holdings") that says that Rifles will pay Holdings so much money per month to lease the machine tools and equipment. Rifles also has a licensing agreement with Holdings that allows Rifles to pay Holdings a licensing fee to use the Silliman Rifles name and logo.

So now we have no property in Rifles, the operating business, but Rifles can still use and benefit from the property, just the same as if Rifles owned it. As owner of Holdings, Sam is free to distribute the profits of the leases and licensing fees to himself. He may also want to use Holdings as a way to "gift" property out of his estate to his kids, as we'll discuss later.

This is why smart business owners don't own property in their operating businesses. There's just no advantage to having your operating business own anything. Those assets just act as a lawsuit magnet to every litigious fruitcake who might someday use or misuse your products. Transferring this property out of the operating business is a way to discourage litigation.

The best lawsuit is the one you're never served with.

Chapter 48

A Bulletproof Strategy for Protecting Your Personal Assets, Too

Don Kingsley's doing pretty well in life. He owns Kingsley Custom, Inc., a business that makes custom rifle stocks. Driving home from work one night at sunset, he thinks about the new client that ordered 50 stocks from him today, all with lots of fancy engraving and inlays.

Don's so caught up in thinking about his good fortune that he doesn't see a small child with a backpack crossing at the crosswalk in his path. He tries to stop but can't, and his bumper strikes the unfortunate youngster, knocking him out of his shoes. Don offers all possible aid, but the child dies by the time the ambulance arrives. Devastated and shaken, Don calls his wife to come drive him home. For days, all he can think about is the little boy's face and the way his poor little body looked lying on the cold pavement.

The week afterward, Don feels even worse when a young woman in a beat-up Toyota Corolla rings the doorbell. "Process server," she says as he opens the door. Don shuts the door and begins to look through the papers.

The estate of the dead boy is demanding $5 million in lost future wages and mental distress.

Don's automobile insurance company, concluding that Don was indeed liable, pays out the policy limit of $500,000 to the boy's estate, and bows out.

Don has to hire his own lawyer to defend the lawsuit. After a year spent in litigation, Don is found liable for negligently hitting the boy with his car, and the estate of the dead child is awarded $3.5 million.

But Don doesn't have the $3.5 million dollars. His business produces about $250,000 a year gross, and the net income distributable to Don, the sole shareholder, after he pays salaries is about $80,000. Hardly a goldmine.

Don starts to get dunning letters from the plaintiff's law firm, demanding payment on the judgment. Again, he seeks advice from his lawyer, who asks him to bring in a list of his assets. Here is the list:

Home equity,	$225,000
Fidelity Brokerage account:	$125,000
Kingsley Custom, Inc. stock:	$400,000
2002 Bounder motor home:	$75,000
Total:	$825,000

"Well, Don," says the lawyer, "even if you liquidated all this stuff, there's no way you can pay off the judgment. I think you should declare bankruptcy; that way, under state law, you can still keep some of your personal items and business property. And once you file for bankruptcy, they can't send you any more dunning letters."

Don's heart sank. Bankrupt! Only dishonorable dead-beats declare bankruptcy, he thought to himself. How could he ever hold his head up again? But he didn't see any other way out of this mess. So he had his lawyer prepare and file the bankruptcy petition right away.

Don's business was sold to another competitor in the industry, and he and Don agreed that Don would continue to work for the company as before. The new owner also kept the company name because of Don's excellent reputation in the business.

The brokerage account was liquidated, and the motor home was sold. After deducting the home mortgage, the house was sold, and Don and his wife moved into a much smaller home. Don and his wife were permitted to keep the "statutory homestead exemption," which in their state was $25,000. So at least they had money for a down payment on another house. But it wasn't like their old home, that's for sure! Still, at least the bankruptcy erased the remainder of the debt, and the judgment was gone forever.

At age 53, Don was forced to start over. All that he had spent the last 30 years building through his hard work was gone, and all because of a moment of inattention on the roadway. It was hard for him to get up and go to work in the morning for a company that bore his name, but that he no longer owned. He felt like the guys he had hired and who had worked for him for years—now someone else's employees—looked at him differently. But at least he still had his job.

Bulletproof Secrets Aren't Just for Business

The sad thing is, it didn't need to end up this way. Had Don done things a little differently, he probably never would have been sued in the first place, and could have kept his house, his brokerage account, his motor home, and his company. It could have turned out much differently.

Let's back up a few years and change the story to give it a happier ending for Don. Listen in on a conversation Don had with an asset protection attorney he met at the SHOT Show. He read the attorney's book and was intrigued by some of the planning ideas that she mentioned.

Don's objective was to deter lawsuits and make himself a smaller target. So he had the attorney give him some advice about how these goals could be achieved. Again, here's the list of his major assets:

Home equity,	$225,000
Fidelity Brokerage account:	$125,000
Kingsley Custom, Inc. stock:	$400,000
2002 Bounder motor home:	$75,000
Total:	$825,000

Don and his attorney go over the assets one by one. She notices that Don has equity in his home that's above his state's homestead allowance (the amount he is allowed to keep if he declares bankruptcy,) and advises that he take out a home equity line of credit equal to the amount in excess of the homestead exemption. This means that whoever sues Don won't be able to sell it and get any cash out, because Don can encumber the house at any moment. He doesn't actually have to borrow on the loan, or pay interest. He only needs to set up the loan account.

The attorney tells Don about a way to use a particular business entity—a Limited Liability Company (LLC)—to shield the rest of his assets. She advises that he form an LLC in a certain state that has "charging order protection" as the sole remedy for creditors of the LLC owner.

In this state, a creditor (such as someone who won a lawsuit against Don) can't force the LLC assets to be liquidated to pay off the debts of an owner.

"Wait, I'm not sure I follow you," says Don, and asks her to explain the whole "charging order" thing.

Don's attorney explains that if a person forms a corporation and owns all the stock, and then gets sued for some personal liability, like a car accident, the person can be forced to liquidate the corporation's assets to pay the judgment. LLCs, however, are treated differently if they are formed in certain states.

Some states have laws that say that if the owner of an LLC (also called a member) is sued, the creditor can't force the owner to sell the LLC assets to pay off the creditor. The only remedy available to the creditor is the basic right to receive any distributions of money or property that the owner would ordinarily receive, just like every shareholder that invests in a company has the right to his share of corporate dividends. This right to "stand in the shoes" of the LLC owner and get his or her distributive share of the profits is called a "charging order."

The trick is that the owner can make it pretty unpleasant and unprofitable to stand in those shoes

So if the manager of the LLC (that's Don) decides to make a distribution of money to the members, the creditor would have a right to get the debtor's share. But what if the LLC manager decides to keep the money in the company? Nobody gets any money, and the creditor who "won" a lawsuit gets nothing.

Why They'll Settle For Pennies on the Dollar

But it gets even worse to stand in those shoes. Here's why: When you are standing in a shareholder's shoes, you don't just get the benefits, but you get the obligations of being a shareholder. Which means the creditor has to pay his share of the taxes on the LLC's profits!

An LLC has to declare each owner's share of the yearly income or loss—and the owners are each liable for any income tax due on their share, whether any money is actually distributed to them or not. LLCs don't pay income taxes; they distribute any profit out to the members, who each may pay income taxes on their share. Even if the money is kept in the company and not distributed, the income is considered to be attributable to each LLC member and taxed to that member personally.

After losing a lawsuit, the LLC (which is completely owned by Don) decides to keep all the money in the company and doesn't distribute to the members the cash necessary to pay the income taxes generated by the LLC.

If you're an owner like Don, you might get a little upset at having to pay income tax on money you didn't receive. But if you're a creditor, you'd really be steaming!

If the creditor wants to stand in the owner's shoes (which is what he "wins" in the lawsuit), then this is exactly where he ends up: Paying the income tax on the debtor's distributive share of LLC profits every year the LLC decides not to distribute any cash out. The poor creditor has no recourse; state law says he can't vote the LLC membership interests. His only right is to get a distribution of profits, if any.

You Get the Money,
the Other Guy Gets Nothing

But what about the debtor, Don? He can't get any cash out either, right?

Wrong! He can still take out *loans* from the LLC, and the creditor has no way at all to stop him. So the debtor takes a loan from the LLC (at market rates, of course) to make up for the money that can't be distributed to him.

The debtor could do this for years, and meanwhile the creditor is stuck paying the taxes, in the hopes that someday, somehow, a distribution of cash will be made.

"A creditor would have to be completely insane to sign on for this," explained Don's attorney, smiling. Don smiles, too. He's beginning to like this and now sees how this strategy could make lawsuits go away before they start, or at least settle for pennies on the dollar.

The attorney explained that you can use LLCs to protect a wide variety of assets, like airplanes, vehicles, motor homes, real estate, brokerage accounts, and businesses.

Why Dump Your Corporation for a More Bulletproof LLC?

Now, Don wants to form a new LLC to run his business, and get rid of his corporation, which he realizes doesn't provide enough protection to his business assets. So he asks the attorney to form an LLC for his business, Kingsley Custom, LLC. He asks his accountant and lawyer to do whatever's necessary to reorganize the business, and they take care of it for a few thousand dollars.

Later, Don has his unfortunate automobile accident, and learns about the threatened lawsuit. Don has his asset protection attorney call the plaintiff's lawyer, Ned Snarky, and give him a little education.

Don's lawyer explains to Snarky that Don's assets are all held in LLCs in a certain state, so they are practically invulnerable to creditors. She tells Snarky, "I advise you that any attempt to sue my client for amounts in excess of his $500,000 liability insurance policy will be of no benefit to you or your clients. You may as well take whatever my client's insurance company offers. Getting any further funds from my client will be virtually impossible. Don't waste your time."

After Snarky hangs up, he does an asset search on Don, consults another asset expert to see if this could possibly be true, and discovers that Don's attorney was right. Don's not a good target for a lawsuit. Snarky is offered $200,000 by the insurance company, and eventually settles for $300,000, of which Snarky gets a third.

Don keeps his house, keeps his brokerage account, keeps his motor home, and keeps his business.

The bereaved family is compensated by the ample insurance Don paid for over the years for just this reason.

Amazingly, very few business owners invest in this sort of planning. And sadly, few general business attorneys are aware of these powerful bulletproof techniques.

Chapter 49

The Danger of Waiting to Bulletproof Your Assets

There are important reasons why you need to do this sort of planning sooner rather than later. If you wait until after an accident or lawsuit, it's too late. And even if you set it all up right before an accident, it can be ineffective. You need to have the plan in place a few years before you enjoy its full benefits.

Why You Need to Plan Sooner and Not Later: "Fraudulent Transfers" Can Destroy Your Asset Protection Plan

I sometimes get phone calls from people who have just been served with a lawsuit who are now (understandably) very eager to protect their assets. They sometimes get a little upset when I tell them: "Sorry, it's too late to protect your assets. It's something that you can't do *after* you've been sued; you have to do it before."

Of course, *before* they were sued, they didn't have any reason to protect their assets, so why do it?

Answer: Because you *might* get sued, that's why. And after you get sued, any transfer you make to protect your assets is likely to be undone later by the court as a "fraudulent transfer."

A fraudulent transfer is the transfer of an asset by a debtor to try to prevent a creditor from collecting against the asset. An asset can be any property held by the debtor.

So if a creditor gets a judgment against a debtor, and then the debtor transfers his motor home to his daughter's name to prevent the creditor from getting it, that would be a fraudulent transfer. A court could force the daughter to give the property to the creditor.

State law on fraudulent transfers varies, but you need to be aware of this issue before you begin any business planning. In some states, it's possible to make what a court would consider to be a fraudulent transfer up to *four years* before a creditor ever appears on the horizon. So you can't wait to do this sort of planning; you have to do it now, *before* you need it.

In a nutshell, the law says that if you make certain transfers that are harmful to your creditors, a court can simply ignore the transfer you have made and make the person who received the property give it to your creditor. In reality, it's quite a bit more complicated than that. But know that any transfers of assets that you make after you have notice of a claim, even if no lawsuit has been filed yet, are likely to be undone by a court. So start planning now!

Chapter 50

Meet Your New Business Partner!

How Healthy is Your Business Partner?

None of my business? I'm asking only because if you own your business with a partner and something happens to him, you may be stuck doing business with people you'd rather not. It doesn't matter whether you have a formal partnership agreement (you should!) or if you operate on a friendly handshake. Here's what I'm talking about:

Steve and John are best friends and have been business partners for many years. They each own a 50% interest in Light Sights, Inc., a company that makes laser aiming devices for handguns. Their product is the best in the business. Light Sights has increased their sales every year over the last ten years, and that success shows no signs of slowing.

Both Steve and John have long-term, stable marriages, and they each have three children. Two of John's sons and two of Steve's sons work in the business with them. John hopes that they'll buy him out when he wants to retire, but John's having so much fun running the business right now that such an event seems many years away.

One fine summer evening, John is out riding his new Harley-Davidson, and a large truck makes a sudden left turn in front of him. John tries to slow, but can't, and hits the side of the truck at a speed of about 45 miles an hour. Despite the helmet and leathers he was wearing, the trauma from the impact is so great that John is killed instantly.

Steve is heartbroken to lose his best friend. John's family is devastated. The father and husband that had led the family for so many years was suddenly gone.

John had drafted a will some years before his death, and it left everything to his wife, Marie. So as his sole heir, she now owns 50% of Light Sights, Inc., and Steve owns the other half. Marie and Steve had always had a friendly relationship, and Marie and Steve's wife Jane often socialized together.

The Nightmare Partner You Can't Fire

Imagine Steve's shock when Marie marched into the office about 6 months later and announced that as a co-owner, she was going to start making some changes around Light Sights, starting with giving her sons Mark and Todd big raises.

Steve sat down to talk with Marie about this issue, explaining that if Light Sights were to do that, other employees would expect similar treatment, particularly since most of the other employees had been there far longer than Mark and Todd. The company couldn't afford to give everyone such large raises, he explained. He showed her the most recent company figures to help explain.

Marie refused to listen to reason. "I don't care. My boys deserve better, and I'm going to see that they get it."

Because Marie owned 50% of the company stock, Steve couldn't just throw her out of the premises. But he had a feeling that he was in for a very rough ride with Marie as his new partner. He offered to buy her shares of the stock, but she refused to sell, stating that John wouldn't have wanted her to sell. Tearing his hair out, John went to see an attorney to see how he could get rid of Marie—legally, of course.

The attorney told him that it would be tough to get rid of Marie, since she was a 50% shareholder. He suggested that it might be worthwhile to sweeten the deal by giving

Marie an above-market price for her stock just to get rid of her. Steve decided he would do just that. He offered Marie a 50% premium over the fair market value of her stock, just over $1.7 million. Steve had to mortgage his fully-paid-for house to do it, as well as put up his own Light Sights stock as collateral. But he finally was able to scrape it together.

He was relieved when she accepted. He didn't understand how he had gotten into such a rotten situation.

This sort of scenario plays out far more often than most people imagine. Everything's going just peachy, and then someone has to go and get themselves run over by a truck. And of course, the person in question has failed to do the proper business or personal planning and leaves a big mess behind. But like most of the bad situations I've mentioned in this book, it can be avoided by a little advance planning.

Even if you refuse to believe that the people that you love and trust would act so irresponsibly, imagine that both your partner and his wife are killed in a plane crash. Now, their son is your partner. Think that's not bad? What if your partner gets married and divorced, and you end up with the lunatic ex-spouse as your partner? Or the dangerous meth-head nephew? Or five squabbling siblings?

Buy-Sell Agreements Protect Business Partners

What John and Steve lacked was an agreement that would allow each of them, under a certain set of circumstances, to buy the other's stock. This sort of agreement, commonly called a "Buy-Sell" agreement, allows owners of a company to decide in advance on the rights and liabilities of the owners if a fellow owner dies, is disabled, or declares bankruptcy.

In any of these situations, an owner might lose control over his stock or, in the case of disability, no longer be able to contribute to the company. The agreement provides for the buyout of the owner's shares in an orderly manner and allows the remaining owners to maintain their control of the company.

Without a Buy-Sell agreement, the remaining owners might be forced, as Steve was, to have as a business partner people with whom he never expected or desired to do business. These business partners might be the children or spouse of the deceased partner, or the purchaser of the company stock at a bankruptcy sale. And short of buying out the undesirable partner or petitioning for a judicial dissolution of the company, there really isn't a remedy for a shareholder in this situation. You're just stuck dancing to someone else's tune.

A Buy-Sell agreement can be written into the LLC operating agreement or the corporate bylaws. If your company has already written these up and doesn't want to change them, a Buy-Sell agreement can also be drafted as a completely separate document. The agreement's purpose is to set forth under what circumstance—called a "triggering event"—one party will be obligated to sell his stock or have the right to buy the stock of another shareholder. The agreement may state that a purchase or sale of the shares is optional or mandatory, depending on the nature of the triggering event and the relationship between the parties involved.

Buy-Sell agreements typically deal with situations such as death, the declaration of personal bankruptcy by one of the owners, or the retirement, divorce, or disappearance of an owner.

For example, if an owner dies, the agreement might state that the remaining shareholders have the obligation to purchase the deceased owner's shares. This allows the remaining shareholders to continue the business without interference from outsiders, and provides liquidity for the estate of the deceased shareholder. This is important, because shares of privately held companies are typically difficult to sell, and the estate may be faced with paying estate taxes, typically due six months after the date of death. So having this sort of agreement solves a lot of problems for the parties involved.

Such an agreement normally sets forth a method of determining the price of the shares being sold and may also provide for funding of the buyout. Life insurance is often used to fund a stock buyout, with either the company or the individual partners purchasing insurance on the life of the owners. So if John and Steve had signed such an agreement, they could structure this as what we call a cross-purchase agreement. Steve owns a policy on John's life and has an obligation to buy John's shares if John dies, and John owns a policy on Steve's life and has an obligation to buy Steve's shares if Steve dies.

How to Fund the Buy-Out

One of the major problems with Buy-Sell agreements is that they often have no funding mechanism. For example, Steve promises to buy John's shares within a certain time after his death, but there's no provision for providing the money to do it. Unless you've got a lot of liquid cash sitting around, this can be a real problem. This is where life insurance comes in. For a monthly premium, the full buy-out is funded without burdening the remaining partner.

The other major problem that I see with these agreements is that they get drafted, but none of the shareholders actually gets around to *signing* the agreement. This means that they paid an attorney to draft the agreement, but amazingly, neglect to sign it. I've seen this odd behavior more than once with my clients, and I just don't understand it. They've paid me for the work, and I drafted what they wanted—they just don't put their signatures on it. I can only attribute this behavior to some sort of superstitious belief, perhaps the belief that they will suddenly pass away if they sign the agreement. Please be aware that if the agreement is not signed, it's not binding. So just sign the darned thing and be done with it.

Chapter 51

Death and Taxes:
Only One is Inevitable

Like most business owners, I'm sure you're concerned about what's going to be left for your family after Uncle Sam gets through with your estate. Too many businesses have to be liquidated just to pay the estate tax bill.

Well, the good news is that a bit of advance planning can greatly reduce or eliminate the tax burden your family will face at your death. You're going to be hearing more about the estate tax in the next couple of years, because in 2011, the amount you can pass tax-free at your death is returning to unfavorable 2002 levels. Here's a summary of the exemption amounts for the next few years:

2008: $2,000,000 exemption
        Estate tax top rate: 45%

2009: $3,500,000 exemption
        Estate tax top rate: 45%

2010:   Unlimited exemption
        Estate tax top rate: 0%

2011: $1,000,000 exemption
        Estate tax top rate: 55%

This is good news only if you're expecting to pass away in 2010. Otherwise, you'd probably be wise to start planning for this.

Given that the exemption is going to return to a measly $1,000,000 within the next three years, if you have assets of over $1 million then you need to plan do reduce or eliminate the tax you'll pay at death.

But how? Generally, you're taxed at death on the value of what you own or control. But there are still some ways to maintain control over your assets while giving them away to your heirs. Let's look at an example.

Ronald Rich owns a prosperous ammunition reloading equipment company, Rich Reloading, LLC. The company employs Ronald as well as his two adult sons, to whom Ron wishes to eventually leave the company. The company is worth about $4 million dollars, and Ron has other assets as well, including his primary residence, a vacation condo in Hawaii, and a very nice firearms collection.

He's very concerned about his sons having to sell the business to pay the estate taxes when he dies, because he doesn't have a lot of liquid assets. He supposes the kids could sell the beach house to raise some cash, but he'd like it if they could keep it, since they've all made so many nice memories there. Although he wants to eventually have his boys run the business, Ron is not quite ready to give up control of the LLC. He's only 63 years old and wants to work a bit more. Besides, he doesn't think his boys are quite ready to run the company without him.

Why You Should Give Away Your Company

Ron comes to me for some planning ideas. I explain to him that under our Federal transfer tax laws, anyone is free to give away (as of 2008) $12,000 each year to any other person without paying any transfer tax (also called gift tax) on the gift. He rolled his eyes and began to calculate how long, with a value of $4 million, it would take to give his company to his boys.

I explained further that not only could he gift $12,000 to each of his sons, but that his wife could as well. So if he and his wife each gave the maximum to each of his boys, the total amount able to be gifted tax-free every year was $48,000. "Are your boys married? Do they have children?" I asked. Ron replied that each of his sons was married with two children.

"Does this mean we can give even more away?" he asked. I explained that he and his wife could each give $12,000 to each of the wives, children and grandchildren, or 8 times $24,000, for a total of $192,000 a year. "So in 20 years, my tax problem will be solved!" he grumbled jokingly.

I explained that we could actually give away far more by leveraging the gift tax exemption through the use of "valuation discounts." Ron gave me a perplexed look. "Maybe you should explain…"

"Well, let me ask you this, Ron. If you were offered the opportunity to buy 10% of a $4 million, closely-held company for the price of $400,000, would you do it?"

Ron thought a moment. "No way. It's not really worth 10% of $400,000, because I'd be a minority shareholder without any real control over the company. I'd offer them considerably less because of that." I smiled; Ron understood completely.

Instead of reducing the size of his estate by giving his children, their spouses, and grandchildren $24,000 in cash every year, I suggested to Ron that he and his wife give each person in that group, 8 in total, $24,000 worth of LLC shares. If we discount the shares to reflect the minority shareholder interest discount that the IRS has approved in these sorts of circumstances, which is around 30%, then Ron can give away shares worth about $34,000 to each of his children, the children's spouse, and grandchildren. So instead of gifting away $192,000 a year, he and his wife can gift away $272,000 a year—about 41% more than if we didn't get a minority shareholder interest discount.

And Ron and his wife don't give up control of the LLC until they give away more than 50% of the shares to the children and grandchildren. So this meets Ron's goal of maintaining control over his business.

And the valuation discounts help Ron when he dies. He will have given away enough of the business so that *he* won't personally own a majority share, either; he and his wife split the 51% of the LLC interests he has retained.

So in less than 8 years, the children and grandchildren own 49%, Ron owns 26%, and Ron's wife owns 25%. That's when he stops giving away shares, if he wants to retain full control of the business.

This means that at Ron's death, Ron is able to value his own shares at a discount because he owns a minority interest. So if we lower the value of Ron's shares by the conservative 30% discount to reflect his minority interest in the company, Ron's 26% share is now worth $728,000 instead of $1,040,000. So in less than 8 years, we've taken an asset that would have been worth $4 million dollars and subject to an estate tax of about $2 million dollars and turned it into an asset worth $728,000 in Ron's estate, subject to an estate tax of $0!

Of course, I had to leave out some gory details, but this is a good, basic explanation of what an experienced estate planning attorney can do.

We can also combine this technique with the one in the next chapter and shift appreciating assets and intellectual property to the children and grandchildren. Combining techniques and being creative in solving each family's unique planning issues can go a long way toward solving estate tax problems.

Chapter 52

How to Pass on a Valuable Business Without Estate Taxes

If you don't already have a multi-million dollar net worth, you probably will by the time you die. And estate taxes will take a big chunk of the wealth you worked a lifetime to create. There are established, legal ways to keep from paying estate taxes. (You really think the Kennedys, Rockefellers, and Gateses pay them?)

But few successful business owners are fully aware of these tools, and fewer still know of techniques that can bulletproof your estate against taxes.

If you're going to be taxed based on what you own, then the secret is not "owning" the assets in the first place. Let me explain:

My client, Hank, has a great idea for a new product, and he knows it's going to be a big success. Hank owns Freedom Hardware, Inc., a company that makes a number of top-secret things that have military applications. Hank has a great new top-secret invention. He hasn't filed the patent application yet, so he won't even tell me what it is. But trust me; it's big. And he's rich already, so he doesn't want to inflate his estate even more by the money that he's going to earn on this hot new invention of his. He asks me what we can do.

I advise Hank that we should set up a certain type of trust for his kids and assign the patent for his new invention to that trust. We can set up the trust so that it doesn't have any negative tax consequence for the kids and doesn't pay tax at hefty trust income tax rates, which can be a pitfall if your lawyer doesn't know what he's doing.

I explain that Hank's trust can charge Freedom Hardware, Inc. a handsome licensing fee (but within market rates, of course) to use the patented technology owned by the trust. This way, licensing fees that would otherwise go to Hank or to Freedom Hardware, Inc. are now paid to a trust for the benefit of Hank's kids, and when they die, to their kids, and so on during the life of the patent.

The income that is to be generated by this patent is out of his estate once he "gifts" the patent to the trust. Hank is going to assign the patent rights to the trust even before the patent issues, when the patent has little or no value. When it does grow in value, the increased value will be in the trust for his kids, and not part of Hank's assets.

If Hank's company is bought out, the buyer might buy the patent outright from the trust, so that the trust enjoys a windfall that will never be subject to estate tax.

Sex, Drugs, and Rock 'n Roll?

Hank likes my suggestion, but he's heard the horror stories about young adult children whose lives are ruined by large inheritances. Hank worries that the kids will get the money from Hank's hard work and blow it on sex, drugs, and rock 'n roll. I reassure him that I can write the trust to include whatever restrictions Hank wants. If he doesn't want them to get any money until they are over a certain age, or wants them only to have money for certain things, like health care and education, then we can write that into the trust. We can make the trust as restrictive or as permissive as Hank wants to. If Hank doesn't want the trust to continue past his grandkids' generation, then we can have it end at some predetermined time and have the rest go to a charity that Hank has already chosen.

The best part is that once Hank sets up the trust, the property no longer legally belongs to him, but he can still exercise a large degree of control over it by picking the trustee for the trust. In order to make sure that Freedom Hardware can continue to use the technology Hank has gifted to the trust, the trust and Freedom Hardware can sign an exclusive licensing agreement with the trust that will last for the life of the patent. In essence, Hank has transferred an opportunity that he has to his kids, at very little or no transfer tax cost.

Intellectual property like patents and trademarks are perfect for this sort of planning. This is because they are literally created out of thin air; the ideas are what create the money. This technique works well for any asset that has a relatively low value but that is expected to increase in value in the future.

Obviously, there's more to this strategy for bulletproofing your estate, but because your company creates and uses intellectual property, then you and your family are good candidates for this sort of planning.

Chapter 53

Exit Planning: Getting the Most For Your Business When You Retire

Ready to retire? Sell your business. Simple.

But who do you sell to?

Business brokers will get you a minimal buy-out price.

Your key employees or kids might be perfect successors, but they can't afford to buy you out.

And the IRS is ready to pounce on your massive capital gains.

This is what "Exit Planning" is all about. And it doesn't just happen by magic.

Above all else, know that you have to start as soon as possible. Not when you are starting to slow down, but when you are in your prime. Most business owners often fail to leave enough time before their retirement date to maximize the benefits of this sort of planning. Ideally, when formulating a business exit plan, it's helpful to create the plan 7 to 10 years before the date of retirement. You'll understand why when we start talking about examples of how a successful business exit plan works. But first, the business owner needs to consider three factors.

Who Will Buy Your Business?

First, business owners need to consider who they'll transfer the business to. Do you have a group of key employees who want to buy your share in the business? Do you have children to whom you will transfer the business? Have you talked with them about this, or are you merely making assumptions? Do you have in mind a company or an individual that might be interested in buying your business for cash?

This is a very important question, because you might structure the transaction differently depending upon who will be buying the business, and whether the sale will be for a lump sum, or in the form of payments over time.

When Will You Retire?

Second, a business owner also needs to consider how much longer they want to work in the business before retiring or moving on. What's the timeframe in which you want to exit the business? If you're 55, how much longer do you want to work? This information is important, because it tells your planning team how much time they have to work the plan that you ask them to create. As a general rule, the more time you will remain involved in the business, the more time you will have to plan your exit, and the more successful it is likely to be.

If you tell your planning team that you want to exit your business next year, they are probably not going to be able to meet all of your goals in that short timeframe.

So start thinking about this 7–10 years before you want to retire. Is it possible to create an exit plan on a shorter timeframe? Sure. But you'll have more success and get more of what you need if you give yourself more time to plan.

How Much Retirement Income Do You Want?

Third, the business owner needs to consider how much income he wants during retirement. Realistically, most businesses won't be bought for cash, so let's skip the notion of a lump sum. Instead, the owner needs to look to the future cash flow of the business—after he leaves it—to help meet his retirement income needs.

Why? If you're going to transfer your business to a group that doesn't have the cash to buy you out, they are going to get the cash to buy you out from the future cash flow of the business. I'll explain this a bit more later.

Once an owner knows how much money he needs to fund his retirement, we value the business to see how much it is worth. Why? Because we need to know if the value of the business is sufficient to fund the owner's retirement, or whether the owner needs to re-adjust his expectations and spend some time improving the value of the business instead. Unless the owner has other significant assets, he'll likely be relying upon the value that he receives from the business to fund his retirement. So we need to know what the value of this is and whether it will be sufficient to meet the owner's goals.

Win Big By Selling For a Low Price?!

This is a concept that most people have a hard time wrapping their heads around: Unless we're selling the business for cash to an outsider, it is most advantageous for the owner to receive the lowest possible value for his ownership interest. Yes, that's not a typo—I said the *lowest* value. That's because the big factor in what you *really* get out of your business is how well you can avoid income taxes on the transaction. And the lower the sale price, the lower the taxes. Let me explain.

It's all about the taxes. If you structure the transaction incorrectly, you'll pay a lot more tax. The problem stems from the two layers of taxes on most business sales where the buyer pays over time. There's the capital gains tax that the seller must pay upon selling the business. Then there's the income tax the seller must pay on the business profits that generate the money needed to make payments to the seller.

Simply put, because of all the different taxes that must be paid, it takes about $2 in business profits to pay the seller $1, and at that rate, it will take far too long for the seller to get paid off.

Here's what happens without proper exit planning:

Suppose the owner's business is worth $1 million. The owner will sell the business for that price, and receive the $1 million over time after he sells the business. He'll pay about $200,000 in federal and state capital gains taxes, so he'll net about $800,000 from the sale. This $800,000 represents cash flow that must come out of the business over a period of years (because, remember, this is not a cash sale).

Of course, the $800,000 is going to come from the business' cash flow, so the business needs cash flow more than that to pay the new owner to pay to the seller. Over the period of time specified for the buyout, the business needs to generate about $1.7 million in pre-tax profits, which gets distributed to the new owners as profit. Then the new owners use that money—after paying about 40% in income taxes—to pay the seller. The seller then pays capital gains tax on the cash flow. Here's how this plays out by "backing into" the cash flow needed from the business for the seller to walk away with $800,000 net of taxes:

For seller to net $800,000, how much profit must the business generate for the buyer over the buyout period?

$1.7 million business profit
<u>−40% personal income tax paid by buyer on bus. profits</u>
=$1,020,000 that buyer has available to pay the seller.

$1 million business sale price
<u>−20% capital gains tax paid by seller</u>
=$800,000 net to seller.

So the main problem here is that the income tax takes two bites out of the money that comes out of the business. Once when the buyer earns the money, pays taxes on it, and then pays what's left over to the seller, and another tax bite when the seller pays capital gains tax on the money he receives.

The two tax bites mean that in order to get $800,000 cash to the seller, the business has to produce $1.7 million in business profit. The result here is that we have an effective tax rate on this transaction of about 50%! The business needs to produce $2 in business profit for every $1 that goes into the seller's pocket! This is why, unless we do some planning, it's nearly impossible to sell a business with payments over time and have the owner be paid off for it within a reasonable amount of time. But if we restructure the transaction, we can avoid some of this tax bite.

A Good Exit Plan Gets You Your Money, Faster

What if, instead of getting the highest sale price possible for the business, we had a licensed appraiser appraise the business at the *lowest* defensible value? The "lowest defensible value" is the lowest amount that we could justify selling the business for—remember that we're selling to a party whom the seller likely knows well (a key employee or employees, or a child), so if we value the business too low, the IRS will claim that the "sale" is part gift, part sale. We want to avoid that because big gifts mean big gift taxes.

So we have a business valuation expert come in and tell us the lowest defensible value. Let's say here that the lowest defensible value is $300,000 instead of $1 million.

Using the lower valuation, the business must generate only $500,000 in business profit to end up with the $300,000 to pay the seller. The seller then nets $240,000.

For seller to net $240,000, how much cash must the business produce for the buyer?

$500,000 business profit
-40% personal income tax paid by buyer on bus. profits
=$300,000 that buyer has available to pay the seller.

$300,000 business sale price
-20% capital gains tax paid by seller
=$240,000 net to seller.

So instead of taking out $1.7 million in business profit to pay the seller, the buyer only needs $500,000 of business profit.

Where's the Rest of My Money?

Wait a minute! Now the seller has only $240,000 net after taxes, instead of the $800,000 that he had before. Where does the other $560,000 come from?

This amount is made up by creating, 7–10 years in advance, a method for the seller to receive money directly from the business after he leaves it. These payments are usually in the form of a "non-qualified deferred compensation plan" paid out to the departing owner over a period of years after he has left the business. Using the above example, the buyer will need about $835,000 in business profits (before taxes) paid out over a period of years to pay the former owner the remaining $560,000.

$300,000 business sale price
-20% capital gains tax
=$240,000 net to seller.

PLUS

$835,000 deferred compensation payments
-33% seller's personal income tax
=$559,450 net to seller

Total payments to seller: $799,450

Why does structuring the transaction like this make a difference? Because the deferred compensation payments to the departing owner are a deductible business expense. They're only taxed once, not twice. The buyer doesn't have to pay tax on these payments before paying them out to the seller. The deferred compensation payments to the departing seller are taxed to the seller as ordinary income. Instead of paying tax *twice* on the business profits that are funding the buyout, the deferred compensation plan allows the money that is funding the buyout to be taxed only *once*.

You can see that if we sell the business for the maximum possible value, it takes about $1.7 million of business profit to buy out the seller.

By minimizing the value, the seller can walk away with the same amount of money in his pocket, but produced from a much smaller amount of the business profits—about $1.1 million in the second example. This means that the buyer can purchase the business more quickly, reducing the risk to the seller.

Why is this important? Well, let's see what can go wrong in these sorts of transactions, and why we want the departing owner/seller to be able to be bought out quickly.

But I Thought I Was Retired!

Joseph Burr owns Recoiler, Inc., a company that manufactures recoil-absorbing pads for shotgunners and riflemen. He started the business from scratch 32 years ago, and now, at age 68, is ready to retire. Besides his home, he has few other assets besides the business. He's relying on the sale of his business to fund his retirement.

Gary Baylor, one of Joseph's key employees, is seriously interested in buying out Joseph. Joseph hires a business valuation expert to value the business, and the fair market value is found to be $800,000. Gary puts down $100,000 cash, and arranges to pay the rest off over the next 12 years, using an installment note. The payments are pretty steep, at about $6,500 a month, but Gary has seen the books, has some ideas for business expansion, and feels he can make a go of it. He's worked for Joseph for the last 8 years and is the most capable employee with the best business sense. So Joseph has great confidence in Gary's ability to run the company well and profitably. Joseph wouldn't sell to Gary otherwise. After all, his retirement income depends on Gary's ability to make the payments every month.

For the first 6 years, things go very well for Gary. His business is expanding, and he just signed a contract to make recoil pads for the military. The economy has been buzzing along at a healthy pace, which means that people have lots of money to spend on their hobbies, including shooting.

In early 2008, however, the economy begins to head south. Gary notices his business falling off, despite his best efforts to find new buyers overseas for his products. As the year continues, it just keeps getting worse, and Gary lays off a few employees to help balance the books. Come the middle of 2009, the economy is embroiled in a recession. Gary is barely making ends meet.

One day, Gary gets a great job offer from an old high-school buddy of his who owns a machine shop. For some reason the friend's business doesn't seem to be much affected by the recession. So Gary makes a phone call to Joseph and tells him he can't take it anymore, that he just can't make ends meet. He's giving up on Joseph's business.

Gary just walks away, leaving Joseph holding the bag for the payments on the equipment that Joseph personally signed for before he sold to Gary. So not only does Joseph not have any retirement income, he now is personally liable for the debts that he thought Gary would pay off as the buyer of his business.

At age 76, Joseph is forced out of his comfortable retirement, and back to work. He doesn't fare any better in the recessionary business environment and has to declare bankruptcy for his business. And because he doesn't have sufficient personal assets to pay off the equipment loans for which he signed personally, he ends up having to declare personal bankruptcy too. So here he is, aged 76, with no business, no retirement income, and very few personal assets—only what he was able to keep under the federal bankruptcy statutes, and that's not much.

How to Avoid Exit Disaster

Had Joseph structured the transaction differently, he could have received the same amount of money and been paid off much more quickly, before the recession hit. Being paid quickly for the business leaves a seller much less exposed to the buyer's mismanagement, the ups and downs of the economy, or any other circumstance that could affect his business.

Some of my clients balk at the idea of doing this sort of planning at first, pointing out to me that the departing owner is actually funding part of his own buyout by setting up a deferred compensation plan before they leave the business. Yes, the departing owner is funding his own buy-out, at least in part.

So why should a business owner take less money for the business and fund his own buyout? Well, because it's the only way the owner can leave the business in any sort of reasonable time frame, that's why. A long buyout period only leaves the seller with more risk the longer it drags out. In addition to business downturns, a seller has to worry about the buyer running the business into the ground, hiring employees who embezzle money, lawsuits that hamper the company's ability to keep paying the departing owner. The range of potential nightmares is limitless.

These are things over which the departing owner has very little control. So it's better to make sure that the buyout period is as short as possible in order to maximize the gain to the seller and minimize the risks.

Chapter 54

How to Choose Your Level of Planning

There are different levels of planning that business owners can use to protect their business assets. Every business owner has to consider his level of liability exposure and his personal and business goals when creating a plan to protect his business and personal assets.

Other factors may come into play as well, such as whether he has children, and if so, the level of their involvement (if any) in the business; to whom the business will pass when the owner retires; providing for a spouse or minor children; protecting imprudent children or grandchildren from divorce, bankruptcy, or other follies . . . and the list can go on and on.

The typical business owner has many issues that need to be considered and balanced—and most of them he hasn't even thought about yet, because they just never occurred to him. This is why you need to consult with a specialized attorney when you do business and asset-protection related planning.

The Basics—Better Than Nothing

The most basic sort of planning—but one that even many firearms business owners don't do—is what I call "Level One" planning. Planning in Level One involves forming a business entity to run your operating business. This protects the owner's personal assets if the business gets sued.

Really, this is so basic that I wonder why so many people don't do it.

On second thought, I know why people don't—it's because their accountant told them not to bother. Sure, maybe forming a business will not result in tax savings. But your accountant isn't thinking about your business liability when he tells you that—he's just thinking about the bottom line on the tax form. To a hammer, everything is a nail.

The fact is, forming the right business entity will provide some business owners with greater tax planning opportunities. Moreover, as we'll discuss further, it helps to protect your personal assets from business lawsuits.

Failure to separate business and personal assets through use of a business entity may result in the business owner losing his personal assets in the event the business faces a lawsuit.

Holding Companies Compartmentalize Your Assets

For even more protection for the owner's businesses assets, I strongly advise most business owners go a bit farther than Level One. Level Two planning involves the use of more business entities to protect business property from the liabilities of the business itself. This type of planning further separates the operating business from the assets used to produce the business income, such as real estate, equipment, and intellectual property.

Even if the business owner has formed a single business entity, allowing the operating business to own real estate, machinery, or intellectual property in the name of the operating business leaves this property at risk if the operating business is sued.

Ideally, separate business entities should be formed to own real property (which has its own risks), intellectual property, and equipment. The operating business can then lease the real estate and equipment from the various entities.

Another entity formed to hold the intellectual property can license the intellectual property to the operating business for a licensing fee. By separating the business property from the operating entity that produces all the liability, the smart business owner makes his business a smaller target for lawsuits.

Protects Your Family and Your Future

Some business owners wisely desire to create a more comprehensive plan that incorporates asset protection, tax planning, and estate planning. They want to minimize the tax bite at their death and make sure that the family business has a succession plan in place in case something happens to the owner. They may want to retire in style and pass on the business to an employee or employee group, or to a family member. This is the type of planning we do in Level Three.

Level Three planning involves using business entities and trust strategies to provide the business owner and his family with other tax savings and asset protection advantages that are not available to those that don't have a plan. These goals may be accomplished in a number of ways, but generally we do this through the use of trusts to hold the business entities from whom the operating business leases or licenses property.

Sound complicated? It's not really, and smart business owners know that they can hire accountants and attorneys to keep track of the numbers for them—this is not a "do it yourself" type of endeavor. And generalist lawyers tempted to implement these advanced strategies without extensive training should be sure their malpractice insurance is paid up!

If trusts and other entities are formed in certain states and properly operated, it can greatly decrease the estate tax burden faced by the business owner and his family, as well as safeguarding assets from divorces, lawsuits, and the financial imprudence of the next generation.

A Level Three plan incorporates some of the same principles and strategies used by the very rich—and they didn't get rich by forking over their money to the tax man at every generation, like families that don't plan.

Is it expensive to do Level Three planning? It depends on how forward-thinking one is. If you could spend $50,000 now and save $2 million in taxes down the road, would you do it?

If you're still thinking about your answer, then this sort of planning probably isn't for you. But for people that value their wealth and want to pass it on to family members and protect their heirs from lawsuits, bankruptcy, and divorce, this sort of planning is a no-brainer.

Chapter 55

How Predators Pick Their Prey

How can a potential plaintiff and their lawyer find out whether or not you are worth suing? Well, thanks to the power of the Internet, a lawyer or private investigator can easily find out everything they need to know to decide if you are an attractive lawsuit target.

You are probably unaware of just how little privacy you have regarding your "private" affairs, thanks to database software and information aggregators like credit reporting agencies that collect all sorts of information about you. What kinds of information are available? How about:

- Details, including account name, balances and transaction histories for your bank and brokerage accounts

- Information about your real estate holdings, including purchase price, the mortgage balance owed, square footage, how much you pay in property taxes, and names and addresses of your neighbors

- Lawsuits and other legal proceedings in which you have been involved as a defendant or a plaintiff

- Information about traffic infractions

- Information about insurance claims you've made

I could go on, but you get the idea. Personally, I find it particularly disturbing that my private financial information is available to anyone with a computer and a few dollars to pay a search company.

Why is all this possible? Well, along with the computer revolution came the computerization of paper records. It isn't that the private details of your life weren't being tracked and recorded before, it was that they were in paper records, which were cumbersome to search and index even if you knew where to look. But databases have changed all of that.

No longer do snoops have to laboriously travel from county courthouse to county courthouse to dig through dusty boxes of records. Now, the records are computerized, and the computers are connected to each other via the Internet. So anyone can sit down at a computer in Ohio and view property records in Nebraska. In fact, you can buy for a nominal fee access to a database of nationwide property records. Just type in a name, and up pops all the property owned by the person, along with all the loan balances, tax amounts, and purchase prices.

Now that our slimy attorney or his private investigator knows about your real estate, they'll start searching for any bank and brokerage accounts that you own. They want to know before they sue you just how much cash you have on hand.

Think that you can trust your banker to keep your financial details private? Sorry to disappoint you, but you have no privacy in this regard. Companies that specialize in these sorts of searches will, for a relatively modest charge, compile a financial dossier on you that includes the location, account number, account balance, deposits, and withdrawals for every bank account and brokerage account you own. In fact, for about $500.00 you can conduct a nationwide bank account search on your target. Basically, anyone with a little money and the desire to obtain this information can easily do so.

Why does a plaintiff's attorney care enough to do all this delving into your personal financial situation? Because they only sue people who are worth suing. If you are a person with no apparent way to pay the judgment that the attorney hopes to win against you, then the attorney has no incentive to pursue a lawsuit against you—it's that simple.

Attorneys who sue look for deep pockets to satisfy the judgment. If the potential lawsuit target has no money, and therefore no means to pay up if the plaintiff wins the lawsuit against the target, then there is no incentive to sue the target at all. So really the first issue that a plaintiff's attorney looks at is: Can this defendant pay? And if the defendant can't pay, a contingent-fee attorney won't take the case, period.

Chapter 56

Structuring Your Business

Most of the readers of this book have already formed operating businesses, but it's never too late to reconsider the organizational structure of your business. Ideally, your business structure will be one that allows you to avoid personal liability for your business activities. However, some business owners operate their businesses in a way that ends up defeating the asset protection that they would otherwise get from using a corporation.

Protecting Your Personal Assets from Business Lawsuits

Some business owners don't seem to realize that if they do business in their own name or using a "dba" (doing business as) they are putting their personal assets at risk. In order to minimize the risk to your own assets, and put only your business assets at risk, you have to form a business entity, such as a Corporation or a Limited Liability Company, and use this to own and operate your business. This is the fundamental premise of Level One planning.

The aim of this basic planning is to prevent business losses from wiping out your personal assets. In fact, this is why corporations came into being in the first place. In the sixteenth century, maritime exploration was increasing. But no one wanted to invest as a partner in a maritime expedition, have the ship and its cargo go down in a storm, and then be personally liable to the creditors of the partnership's venture for the lost cargo.

Wanting to encourage exploration and the establishment of overseas colonies, the British Crown permitted the charter of corporations, so that the risks of the venture were limited only to the amount an investor invested. No longer at risk to the amount of everything they owned, investors were more likely to put up capital for maritime exploration.

Here's how this works. Instead of doing business in your own name, you form an entity in the state in which you will be conducting your business. You file Articles of Incorporation with the Secretary of State's office, pay a fee, and create Bylaws stating how the corporation will be run. You open up a corporate bank account to separate the corporation's money from your money. Voila! You've done it!

Keep it Separated!

This last bit about separating your own money from that of the corporation is pretty important, but too many business owners get sloppy about it. A client of mine once admitted to me that he used his corporation as sort of a personal piggy bank. He used the corporate account to pay his personal mortgage, to buy a new car, and to pay for most of his living expenses.

He stopped treating this so lightly when I told him that by doing this, he was endangering his personal assets in the event one of his products malfunctioned and caused the company to be sued.

Why would his personal assets be put at risk by his behavior? Because if you treat the corporation as your personal piggy bank, a court will figure, when it's time to hold your corporation liable for some wrong, that if you didn't respect the corporation's money as the corporation's, then why should anyone else? In a situation where the major shareholder is treating the company money as his own, isn't it fair to also treat the debts as his too? The courts think so. If you want the corporate entity to be respected, it must be separate from the shareholders, and not merely an alter ego. So watch out for this. If you need money from your corporation, take out a loan. Don't treat the corporate bank account like a personal slush fund.

Don't Get Pierced!

How else might you as an owner be held personally liable for the debts of the corporation? Well, let's look at some more justifications for "piercing the corporate veil."

The failure to follow corporate formalities is often used as an excuse to pierce the corporate veil and hold the corporation's shareholders liable for the corporation's debts. Most state laws require a corporation to have an annual meeting and keep minutes of the annual meeting. Many small businesses seriously neglect this requirement. I have a client who, after getting sued by a large university, realized that they had no minutes of their annual meetings for the previous 12 years. Yes, that's right—12 years! And this while the company was making gobs of money. They were so busy making gobs of money that they didn't take care of this small but important detail. They paid me a significant sum to correct this for them. They're now paying more attention to this detail.

If the major shareholder of the business is siphoning off assets, that's another reason to pierce the corporate veil. Let's say Sam and his family own a business, but Sam is the major stockholder, owning 55% of the total stock, and the rest of the family owns the other 45%. Sam is the only person involved in the day-to-day operations, so he pretty much does whatever he wants, and the other family members go along with whatever Sam proposes at their annual board meetings. Sam takes money out of the corporation to fund his pet hobby, which is paragliding. He uses corporate funds to pay for trips and to purchase the latest and greatest paragliders. Watch out, Sam! Keep on doing that, and treating the corporation as your own personal piggy bank, and you'll make yourself and the other shareholders liable for the debts of the corporation, even if you're the one doing the siphoning, and even if you don't own all the company stock.

Another reason commonly used to pierce the corporate veil is that the corporation failed to maintain "arm's length" relationships with related entities. For example, if your corporation is leasing property and equipment from another entity that you also own, it needs to be documented by a lease agreement, and lease amount needs to reflect a market rate for the property leased.

You need to understand that when a court looks to pierce the corporate veil, it doesn't look at each factor in isolation, but rather at the whole situation. Minor problems with recordkeeping are not going to result in piercing the corporate veil if the corporation or LLC is otherwise being properly run. As an aside, another reason why I like LLCs rather than corporations is because an LLC has fewer corporate formalities required by state law. So fewer required formalities means fewer formalities to mess up or forget. Consider this as a factor when deciding which sort of entity to form to run your business.

Chapter 57

Selecting a Business Planning and Asset Protection Attorney

Unlike attorneys who specialize in patents and trademarks, attorneys who specialize in asset protection planning and business planning don't have specialized designations. To become a patent attorney, you have to pass a special examination given by the U.S. Patent and Trademark Office.

To specialize in asset protection planning and business planning, you merely have to claim the specialty. So how does the average consumer know how to hire the right person to help them plan in this very complex area? Asking the right questions helps. For example, how long have they been practicing in the field, and what portion of their practice is devoted to asset protection, estate, and business planning?

For an attorney to be a genuine expert in this field, their practice should be devoted exclusively to this area. Why? Because this area of the law is so complex that an attorney that includes other areas of law in his practice is not going to be able to keep up with what's going on the asset protection, estate, and business planning arena.

The Yellow Pages is probably the worst place to pick an attorney to do complex estate, business, or asset protection planning. This is because most attorneys with large ads in the Yellow Pages will take whatever comes in the door. They don't really specialize in anything. Sure, they'll tell you that they do estate planning, but this may mean that they've written a simple will or two. However, they'll be unlikely to have the knowledge of the estate and gift tax laws sufficient to draft a comprehensive estate plan. I've seen too many inexperienced estate planners cause too many disastrous problems for their clients. The worst part about it is that the client didn't know about the problems until they died. By then, it's too late to fix it.

Hiring a big firm to do your planning is no guarantee of success, either. I once reviewed an estate plan done by a very large and well-respected law firm in Texas. Because the documents used the word "general" instead of the word "specific" in one very critical sentence, the family ended up paying over $1 million *extra* in estate tax at the death of the children of the client. I'm not sure whether the attorney that drafted the documents just didn't know any better, or whether he wasn't thinking about the family tax bill for the future generations. But it cost my client an awful lot of money.

Sometimes my clients have hesitated before hiring me because I'm not licensed to practice law in their particular state. I explain to them that drafting an operating agreement using a particular state's law isn't necessarily considered the practice of law in most states. I have a couple of states which I favor for forming businesses, and I'm licensed to practice in those. If a particular state law comes up and I need to know more about it, I know qualified specialists all over the country whom I can call upon to assist.

Working long distance is rarely a concern. I work with clients from all over the country who want to plan and who don't mind chatting on the phone with me. Sometimes I'll fly out to see them, or they'll come to the Lake Tahoe area, and combine a vacation with a visit to me.

I am often asked by my clients, "How much will it cost?" That's a difficult question for me to answer before I've had a chance to talk with the client. I haven't any idea what their situation is until I talk to them, nor what their goals or particular concerns are. Most attorneys able to provide this type of sophisticated planning will expect a consultation fee to meet initially with the client; this is not the type of thing for which one should expect a "free consultation." No serious business owner would expect to get free advice from an attorney and then try to find a cheaper attorney to try to implement the plan, so you won't find most attorneys of this caliber giving their time away for free. After the attorney understands the scope of the work, they can give you a fee quote. Most of this type of work is done on a flat-fee basis for the client, and hourly fees are generally avoided. Generally, fees reflect the complexity of the work and the projected tax savings to the client.

The Opportunities to Protect Your Wealth are Profound—the Time to Begin Planning is Now

We've discussed some very valuable planning ideas for your business, but until an owner takes responsibility for his business and puts a plan into action, there is nothing a planner can do to help him. If you feel that you have some vulnerabilities like the characters in the stories I used as examples, then I urge you to call a competent lawyer to discuss how he or she might be able to plan to help you sleep easier at night.

To Receive Updates

Because the law changes, and future editions of this book will undoubtedly have improvements based on reader feedback and questions, we invite you to sign up for occasional email updates at:

www.BulletproofFirearmsBusiness.com

Clients needing additional copies of this book for key employees and outside marketing and advertising contractors may contact the authors for special consideration.